Delightful Journeys

A Coloring Book for Everyone

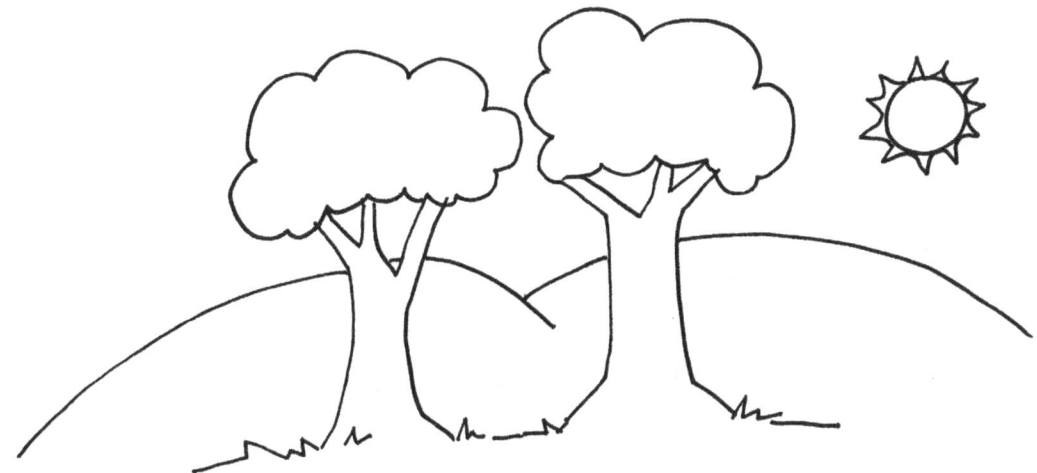

By Kimberly Garvey

Cover Drawing By Kimberly Garvey

Cover Drawing Colored By Donna Pecoraro

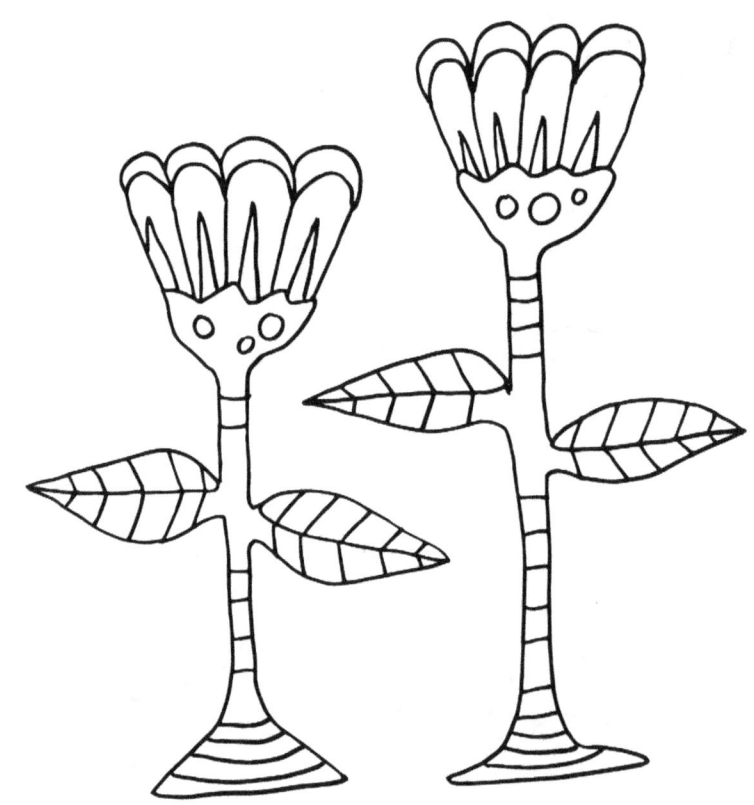

Smiling Bat Productions

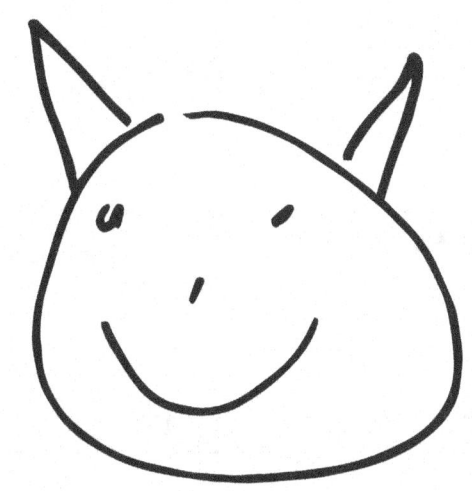

This book is dedicated to everyone I love.

WARNING!!!!

Please put a protection sheet of paper between the pages when using markers to prevent bleed-through.

A protection sheet is included at the back of

this

book.

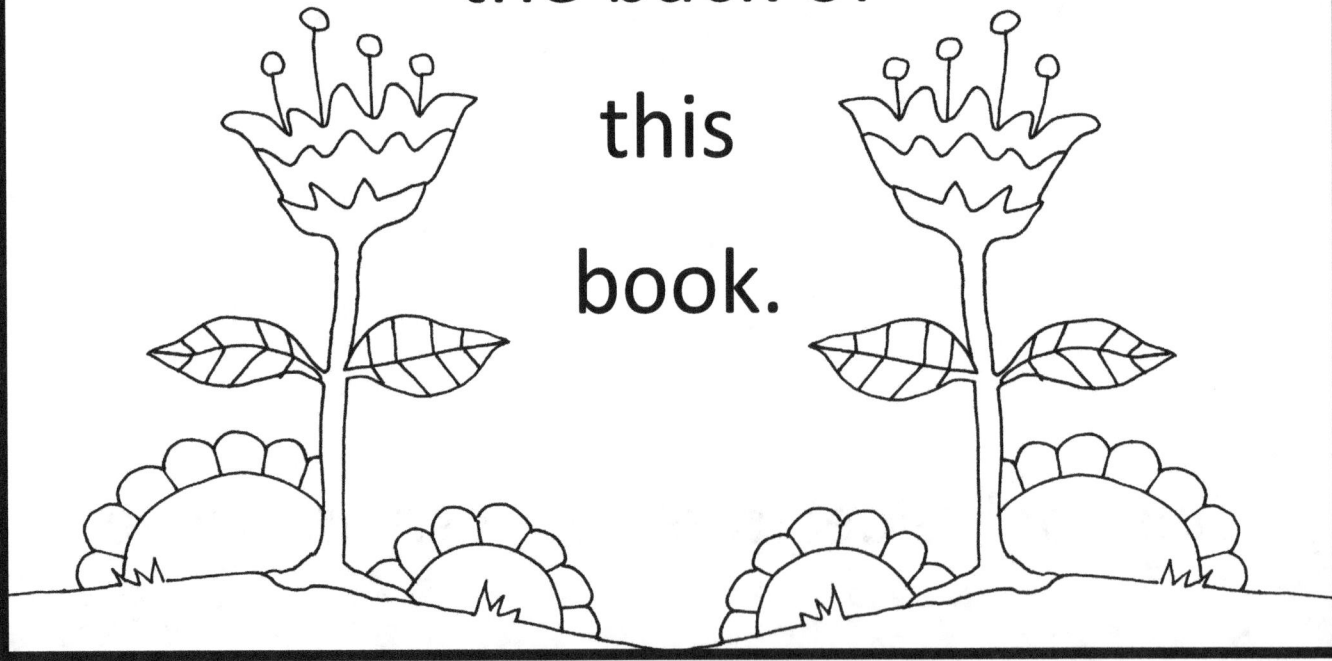

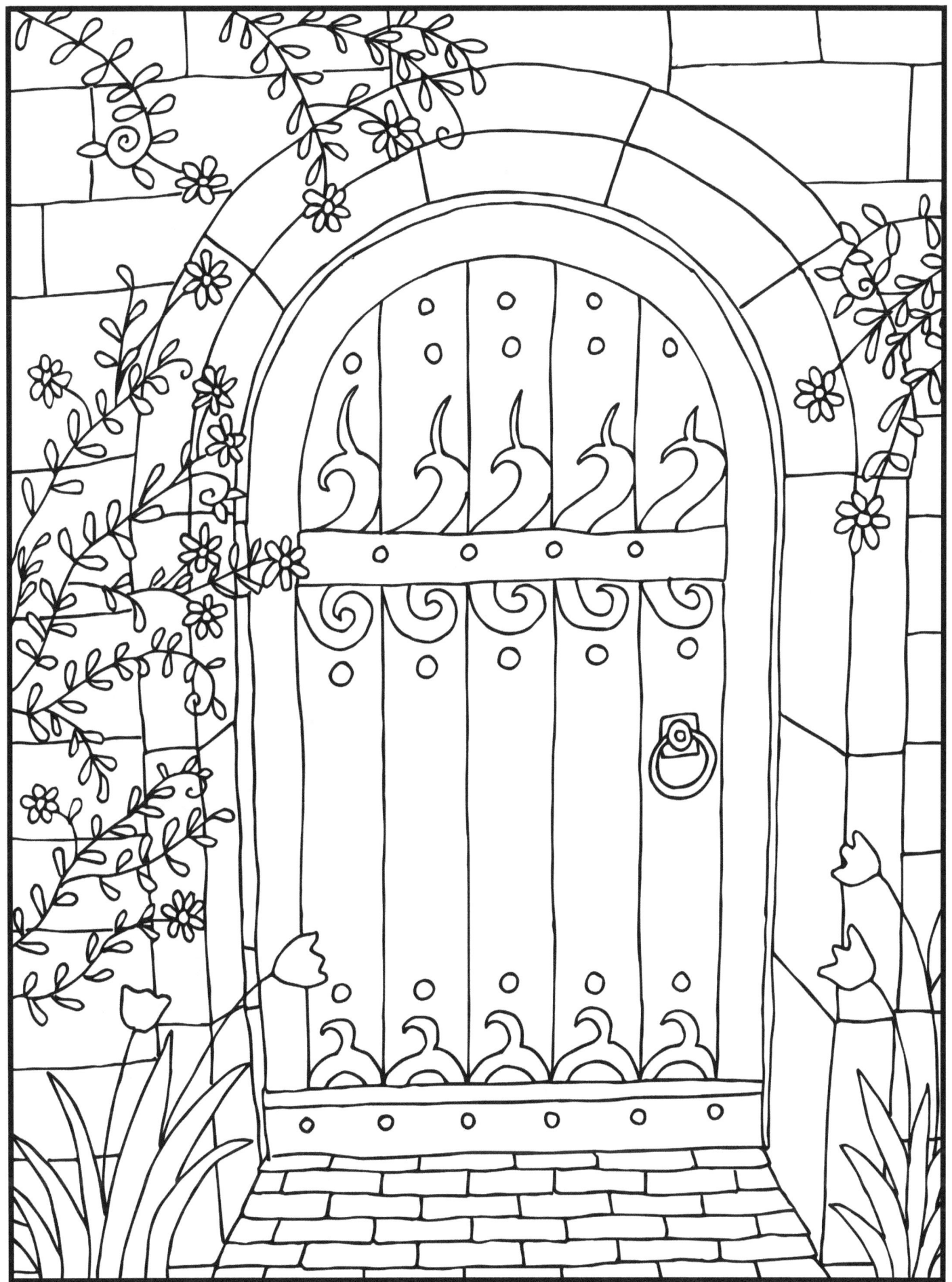

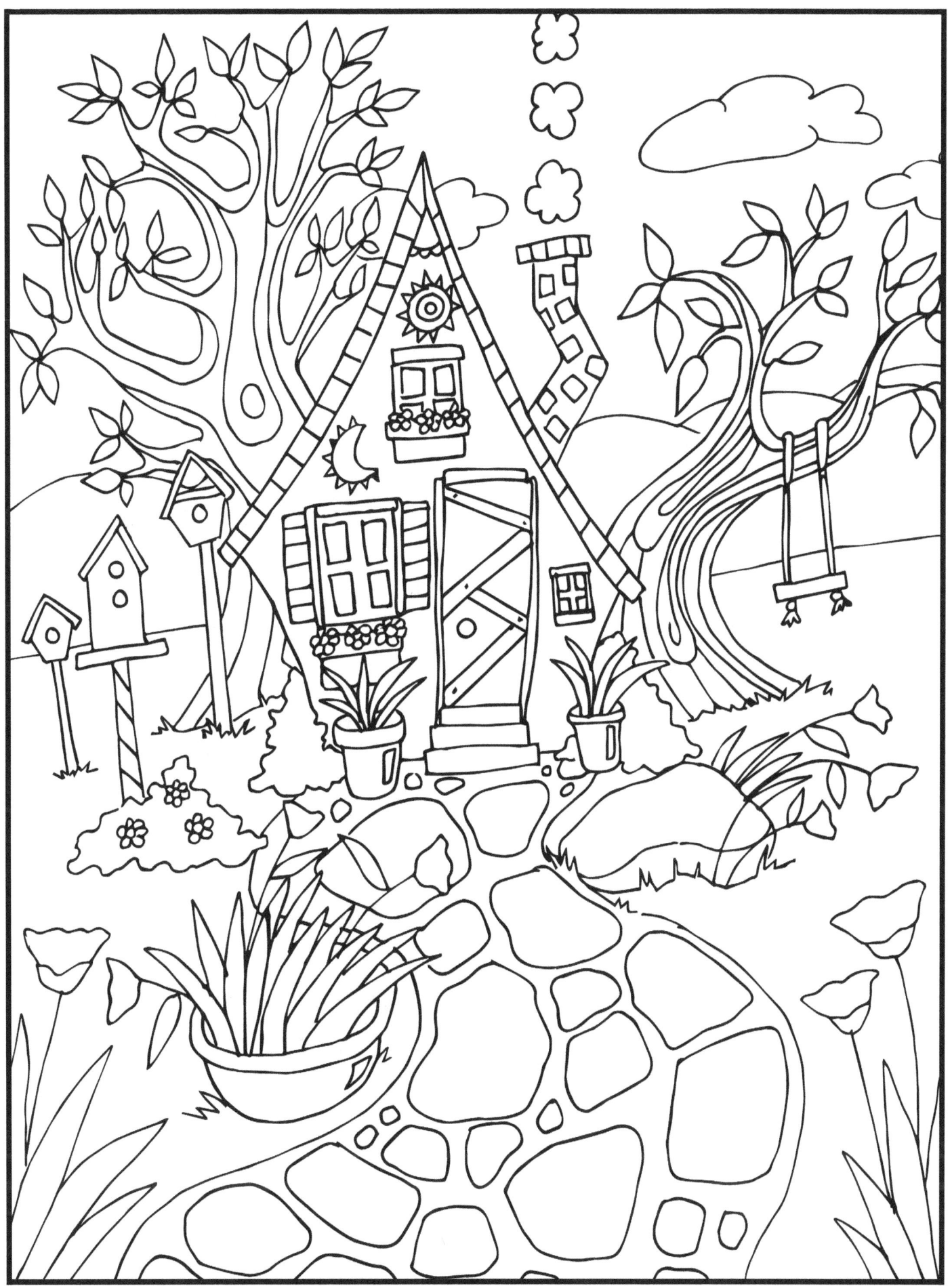

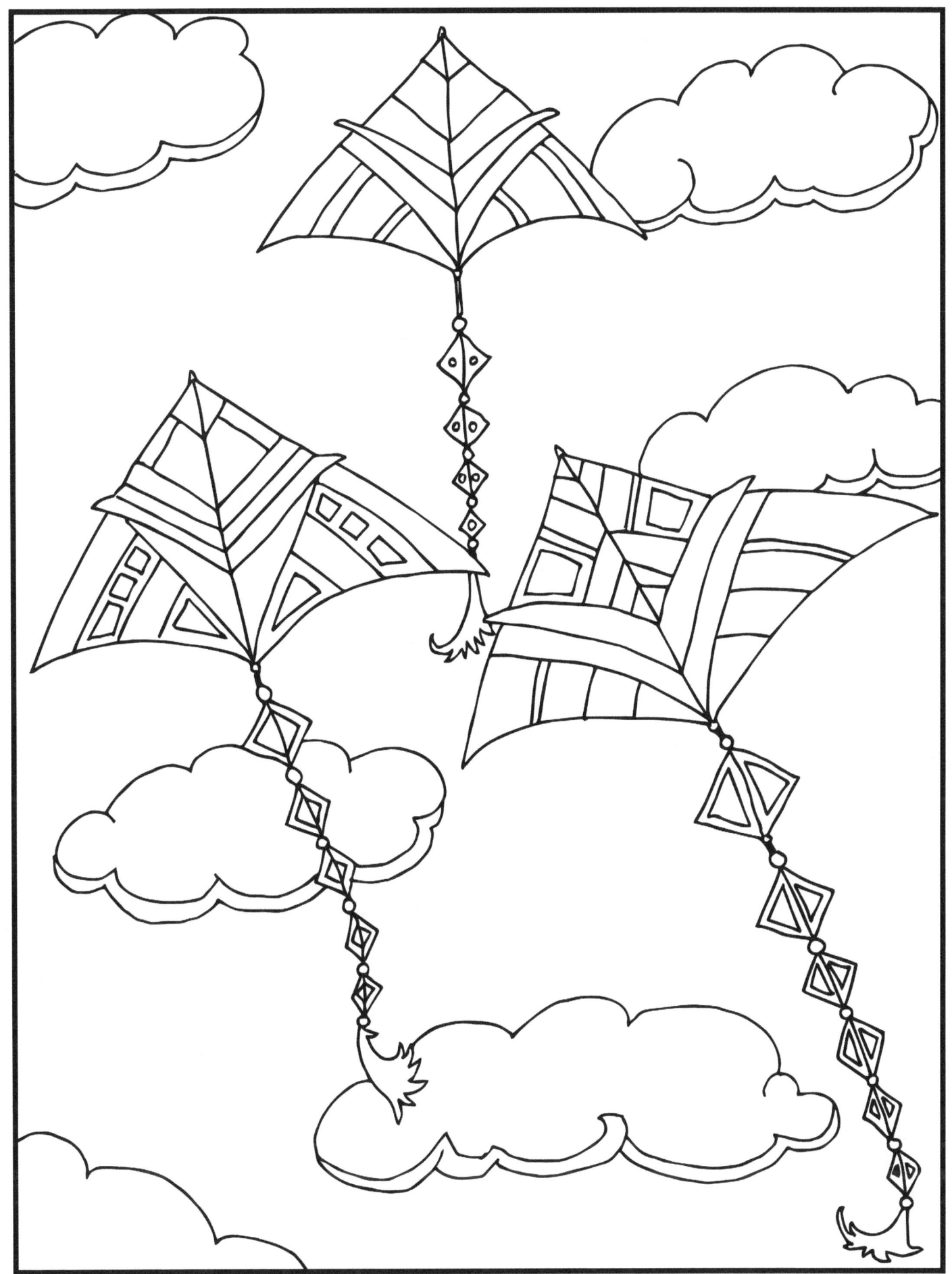

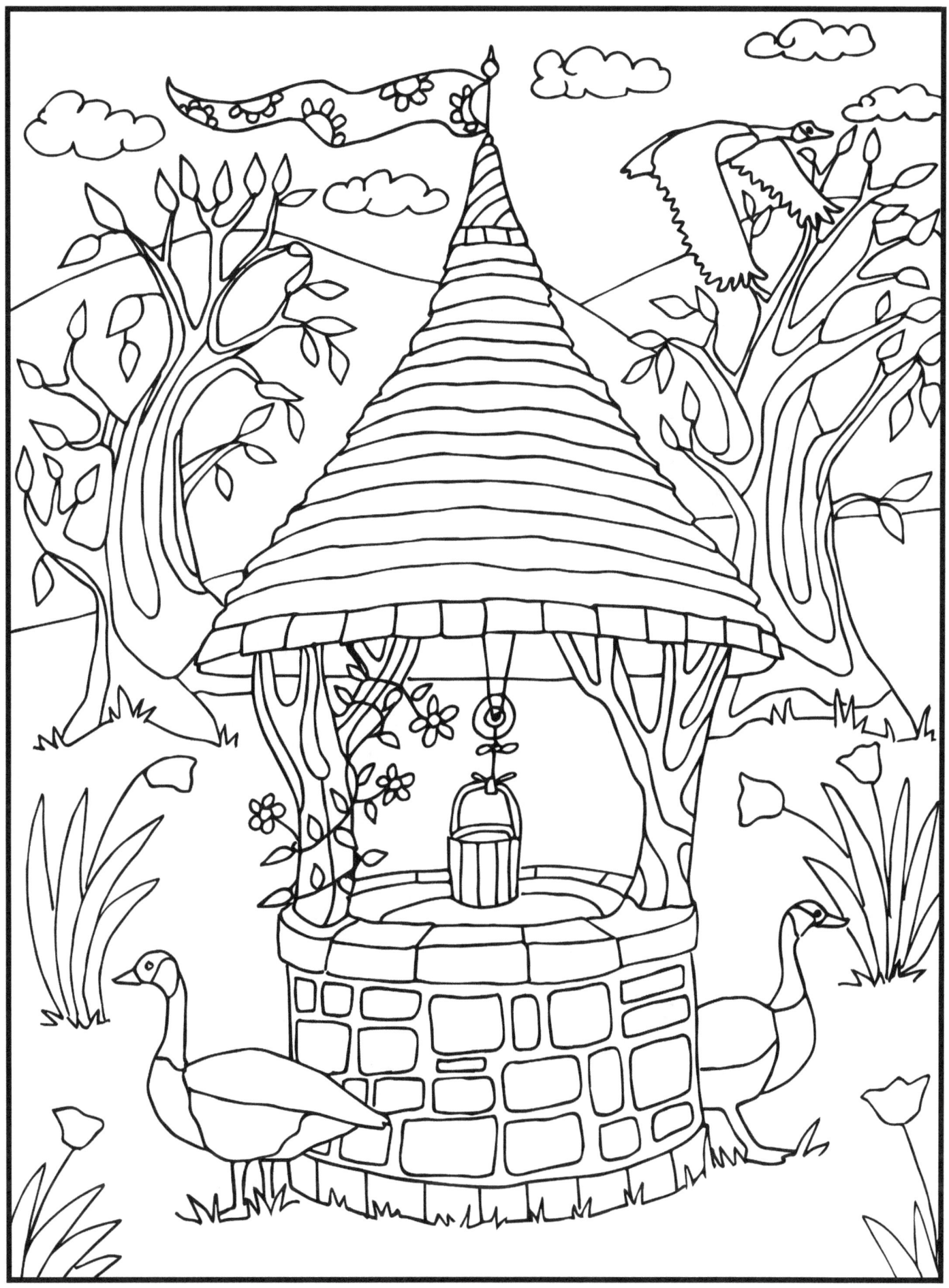

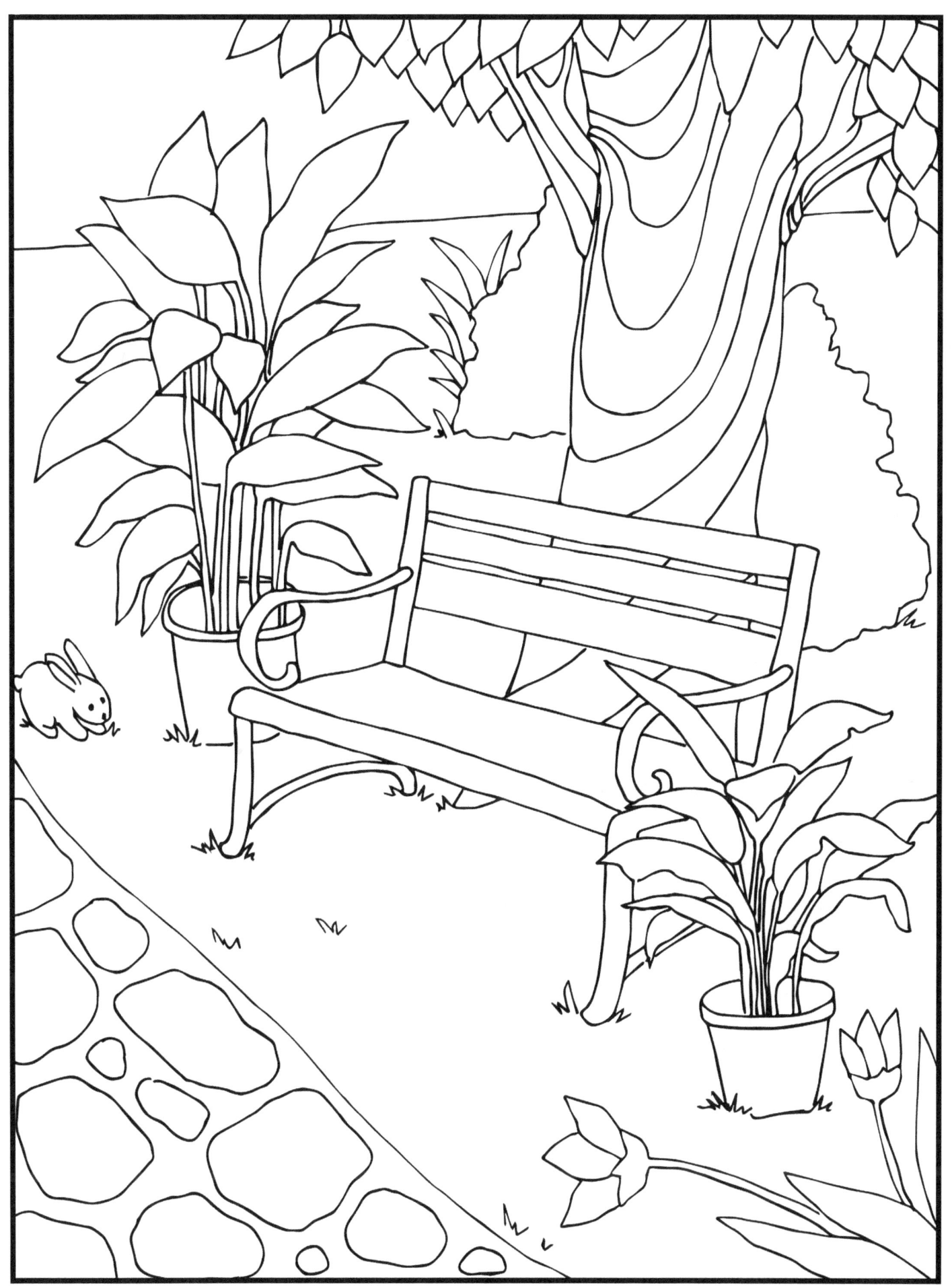

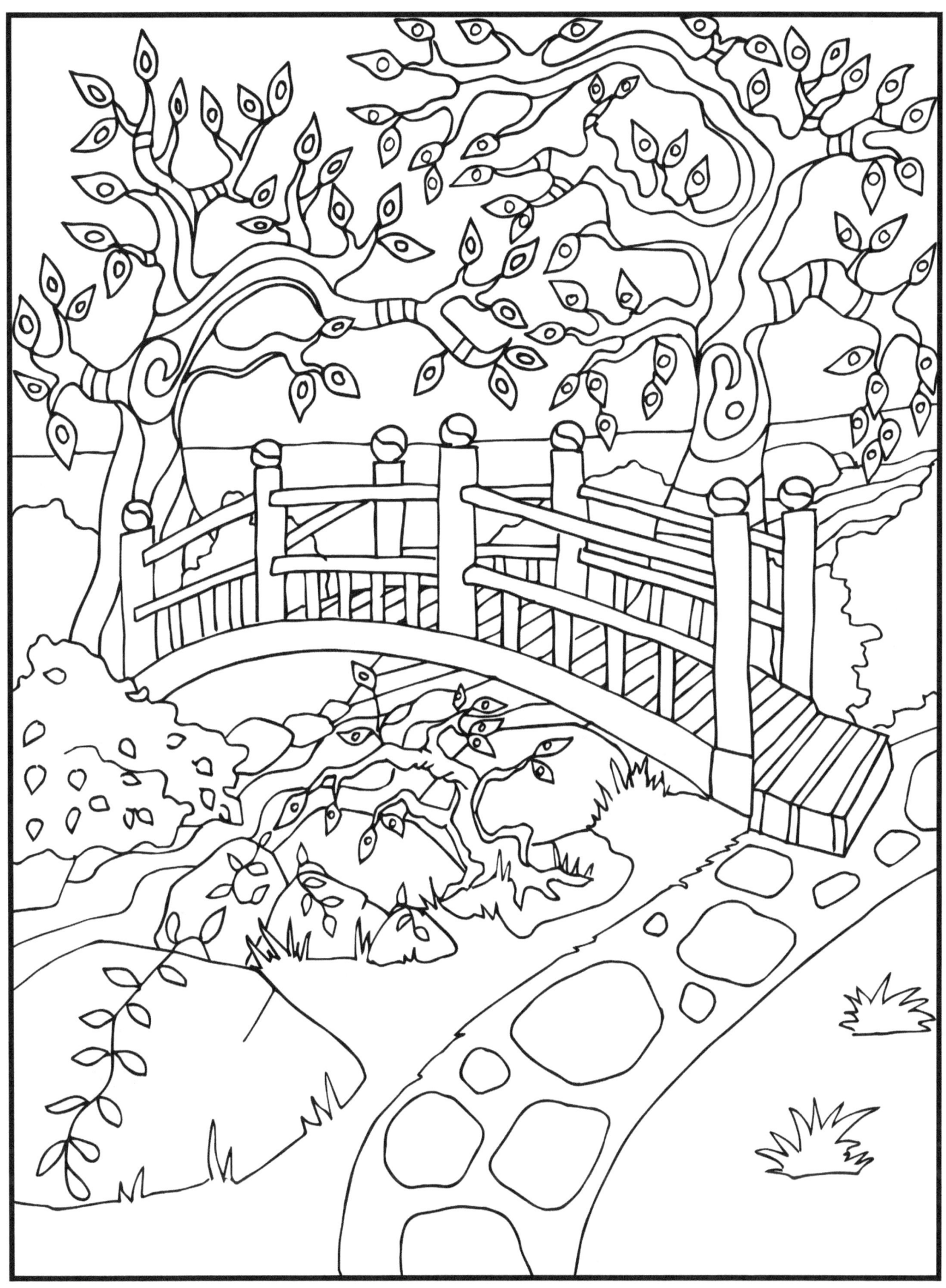

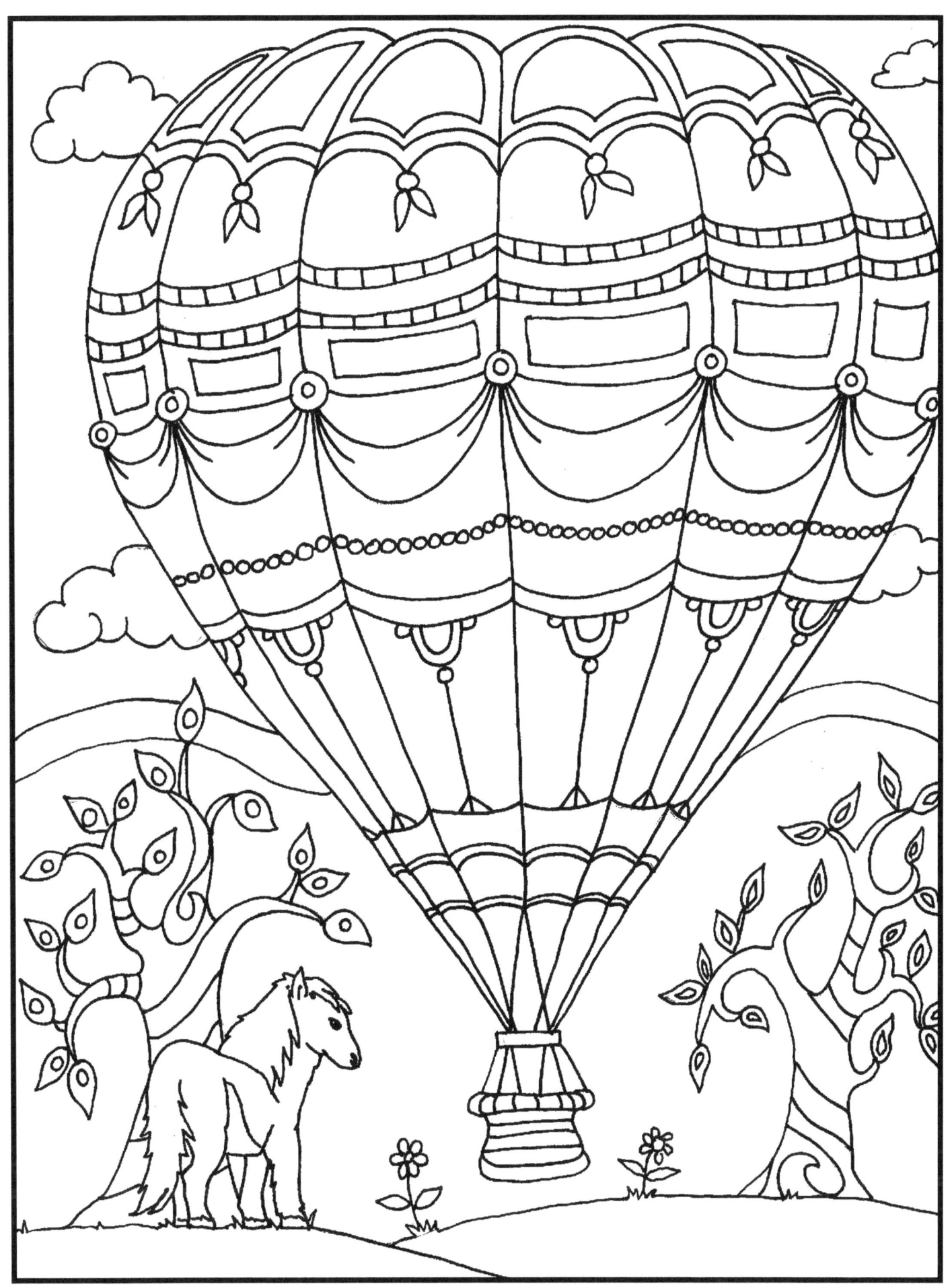

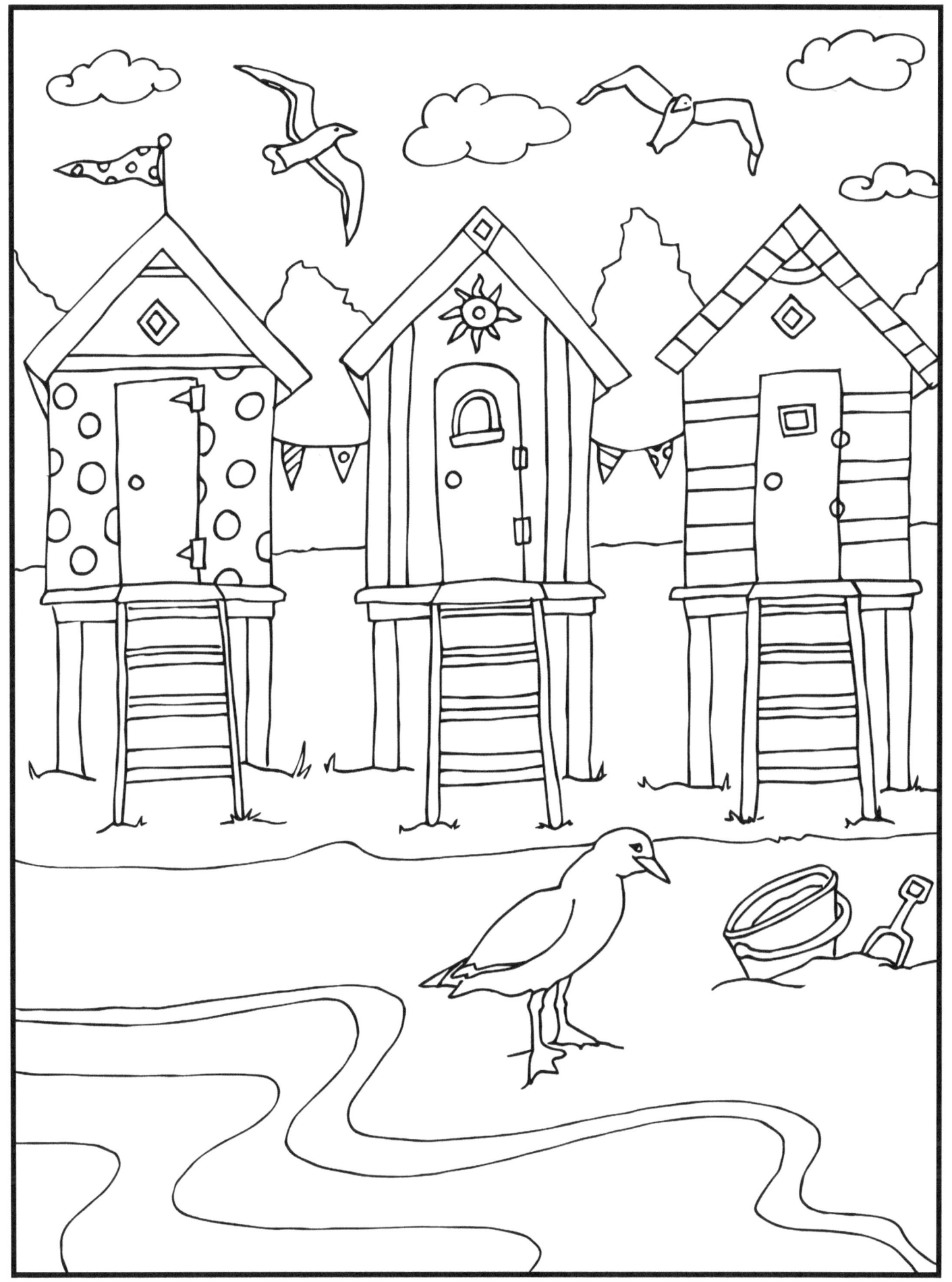

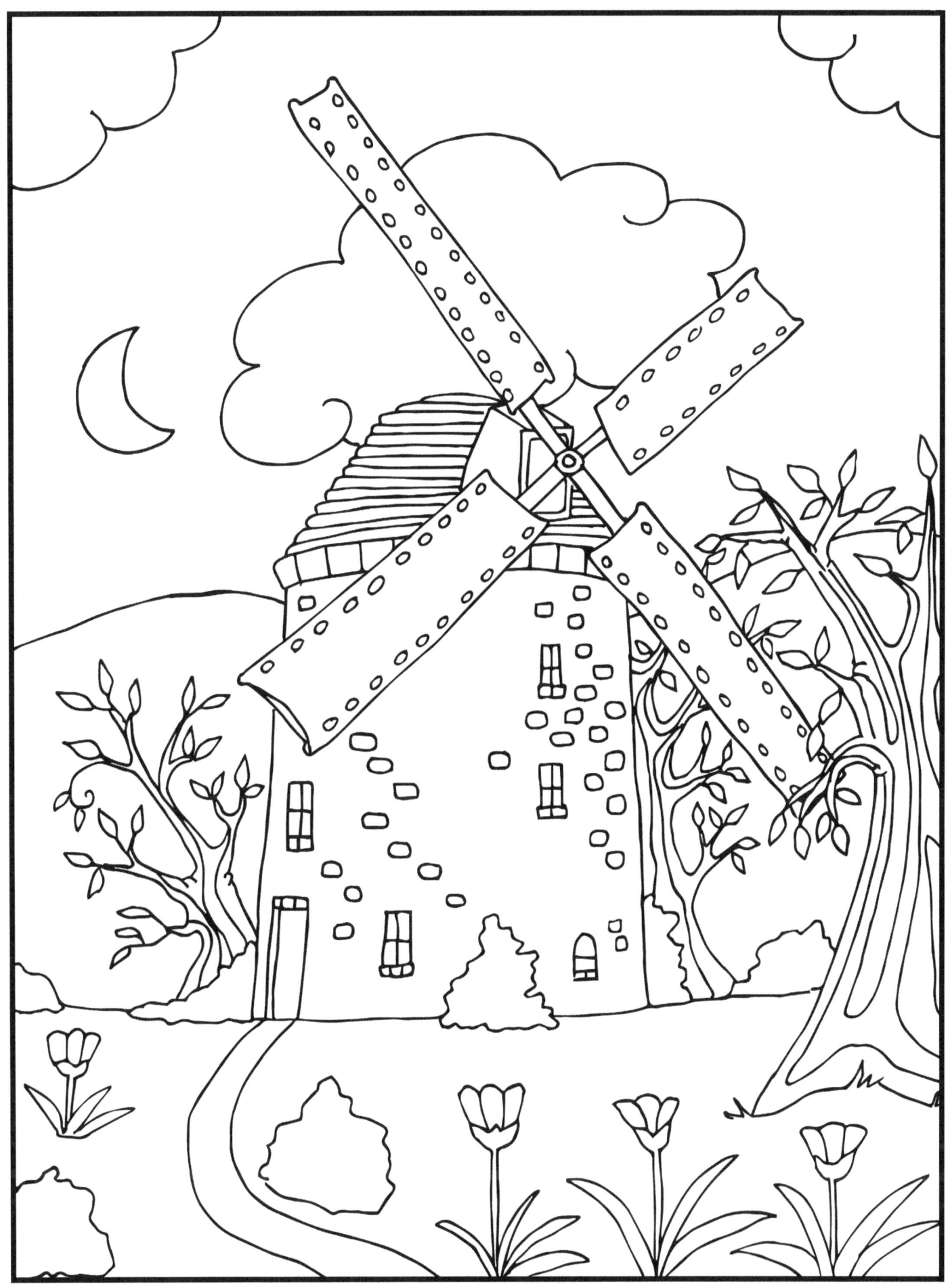

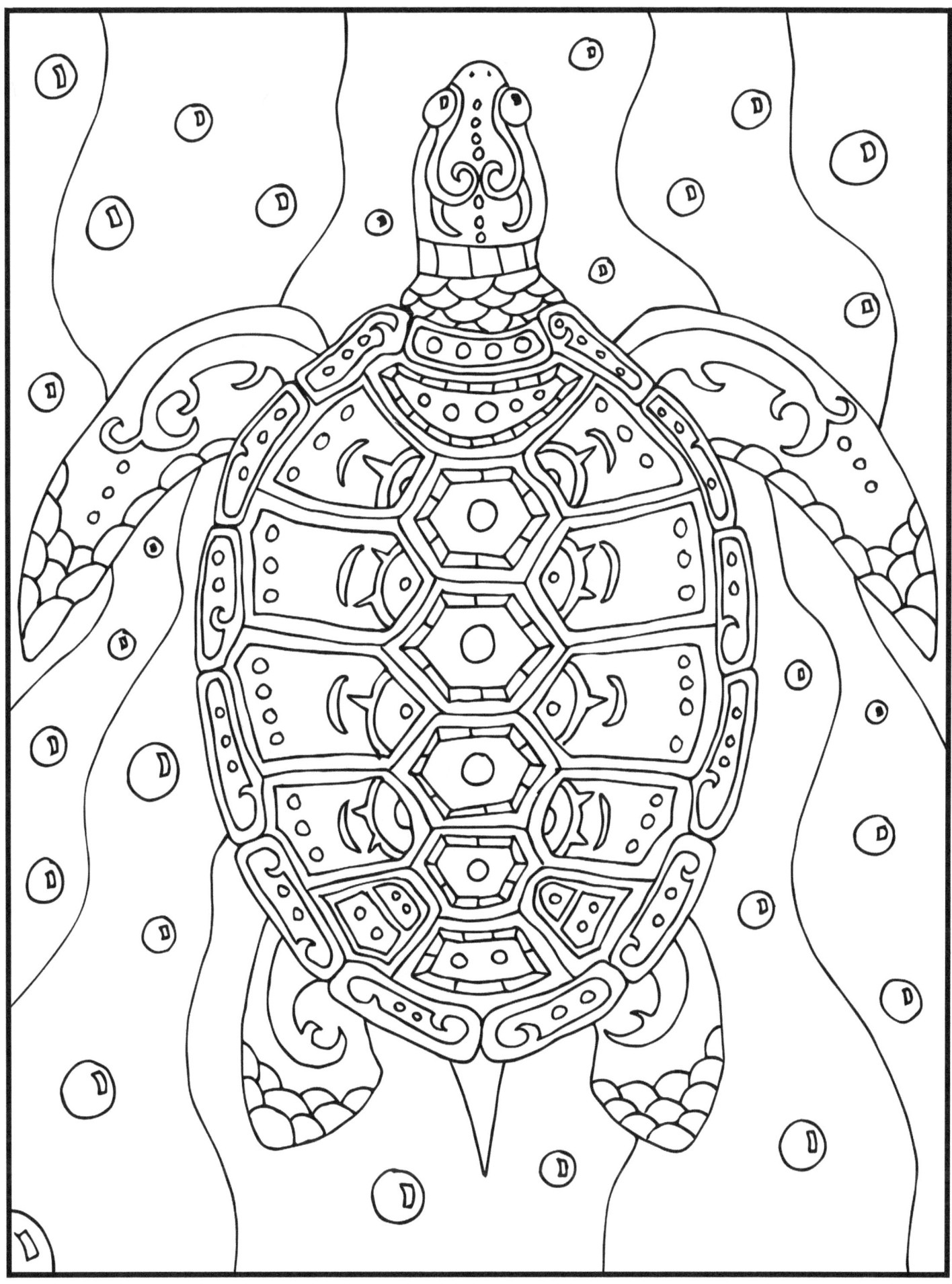

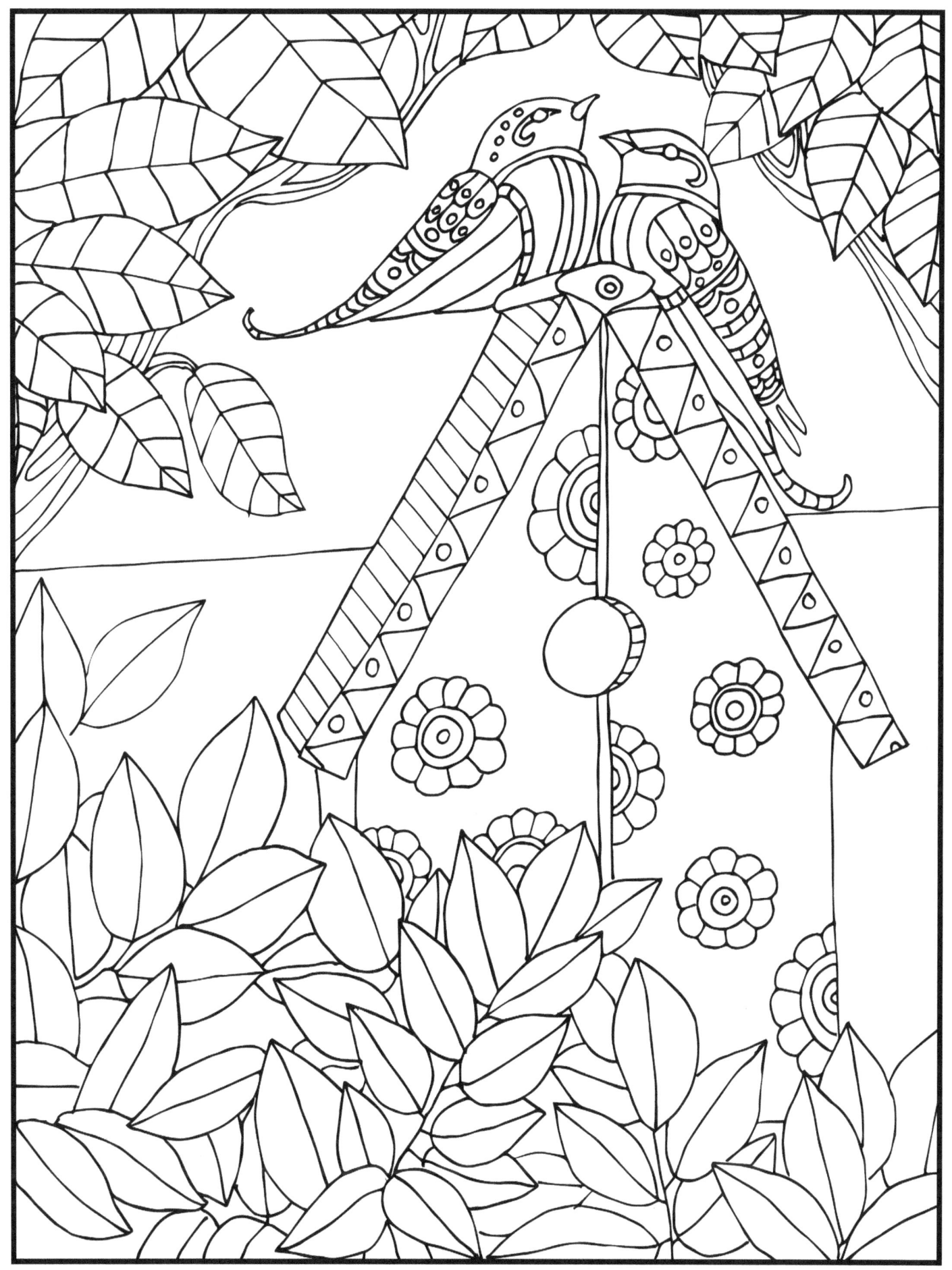

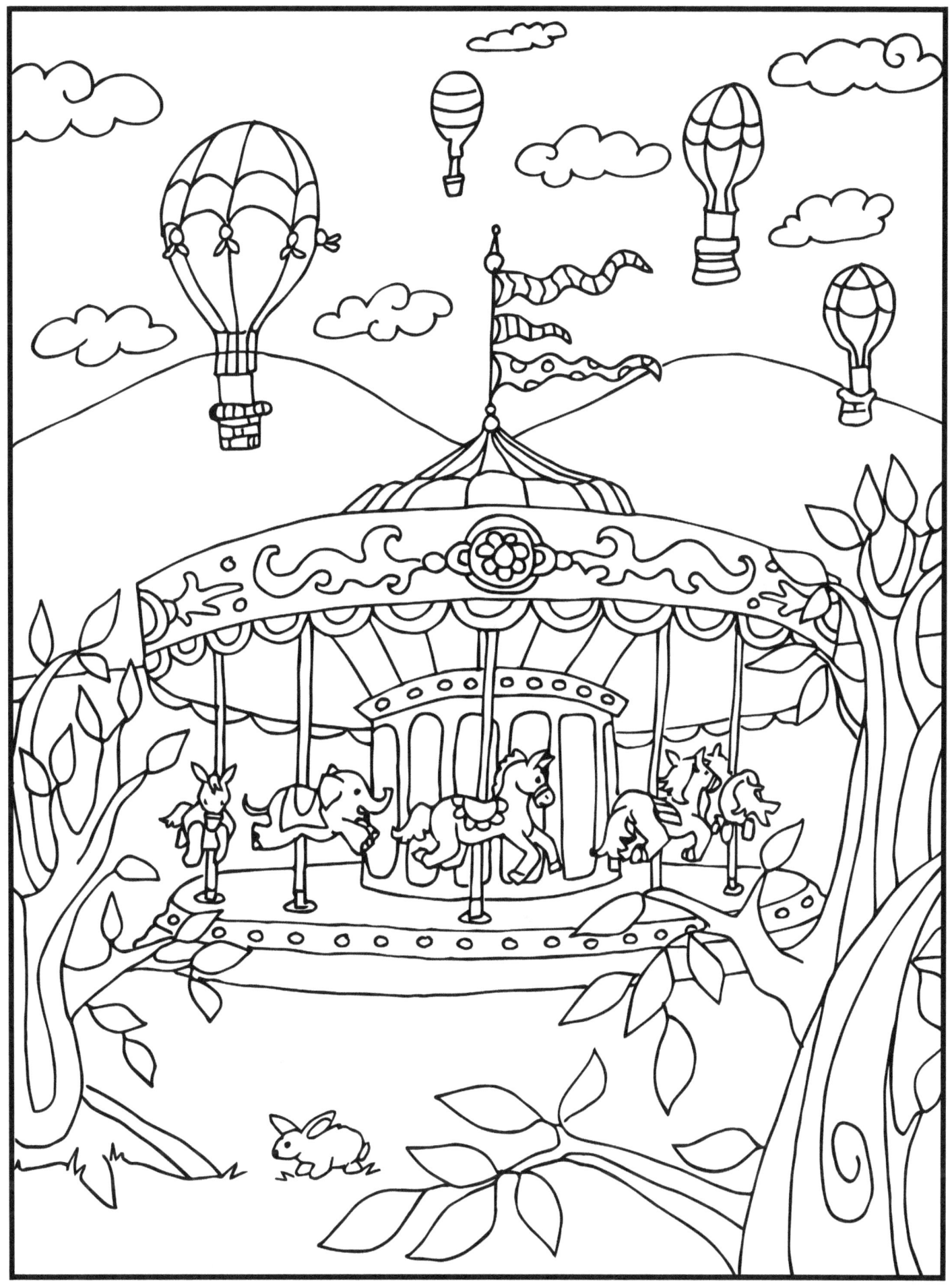

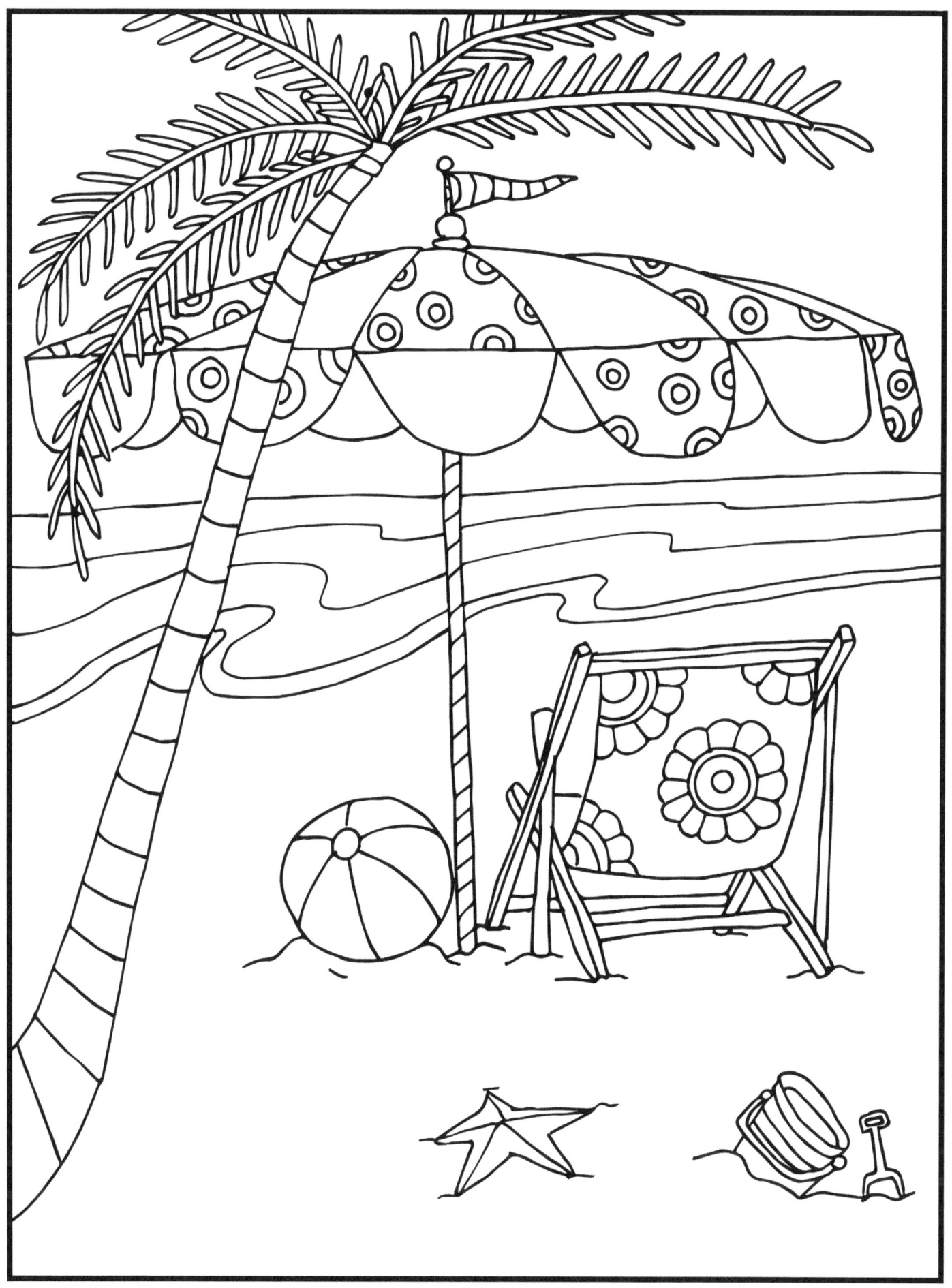

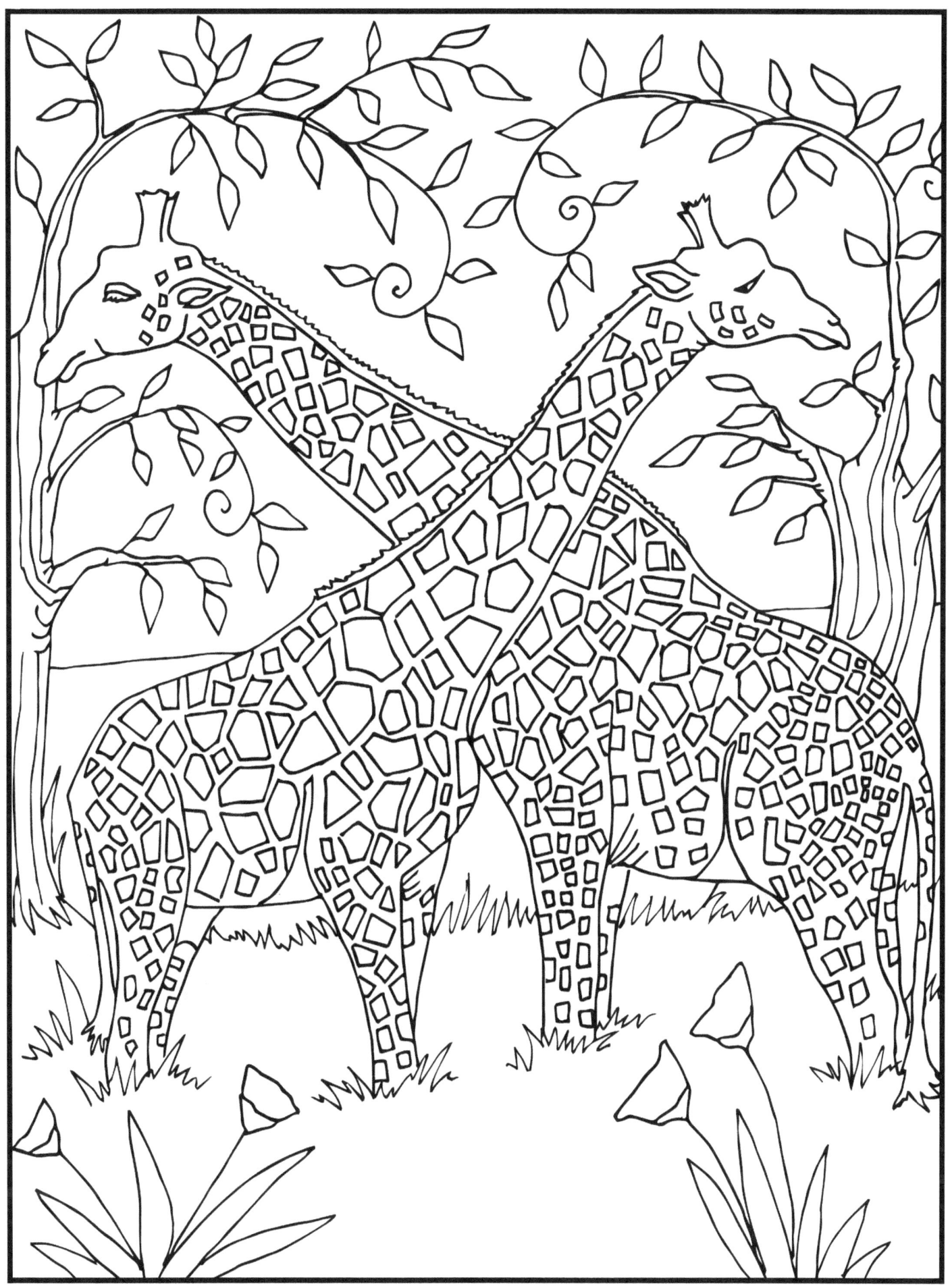

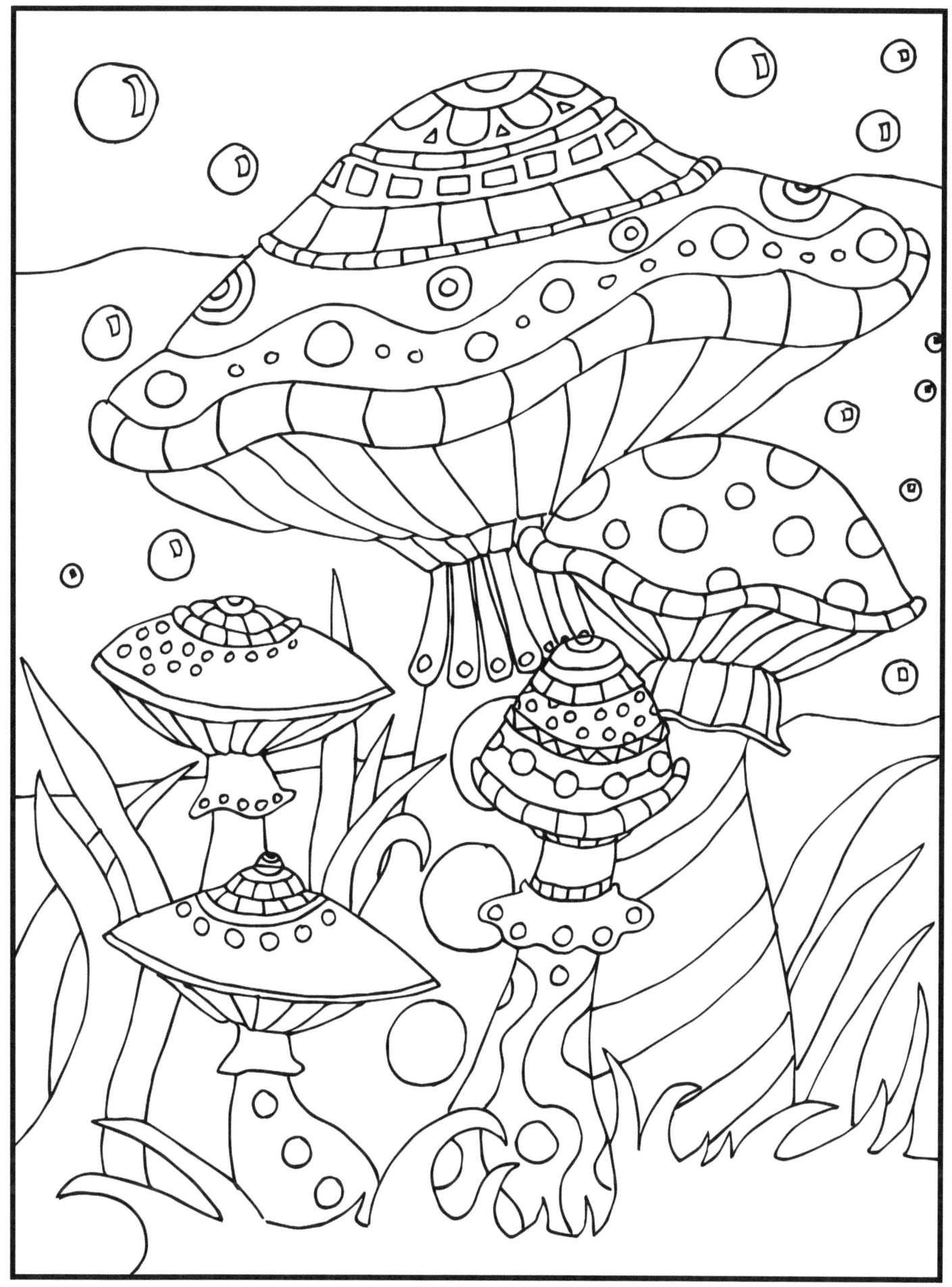

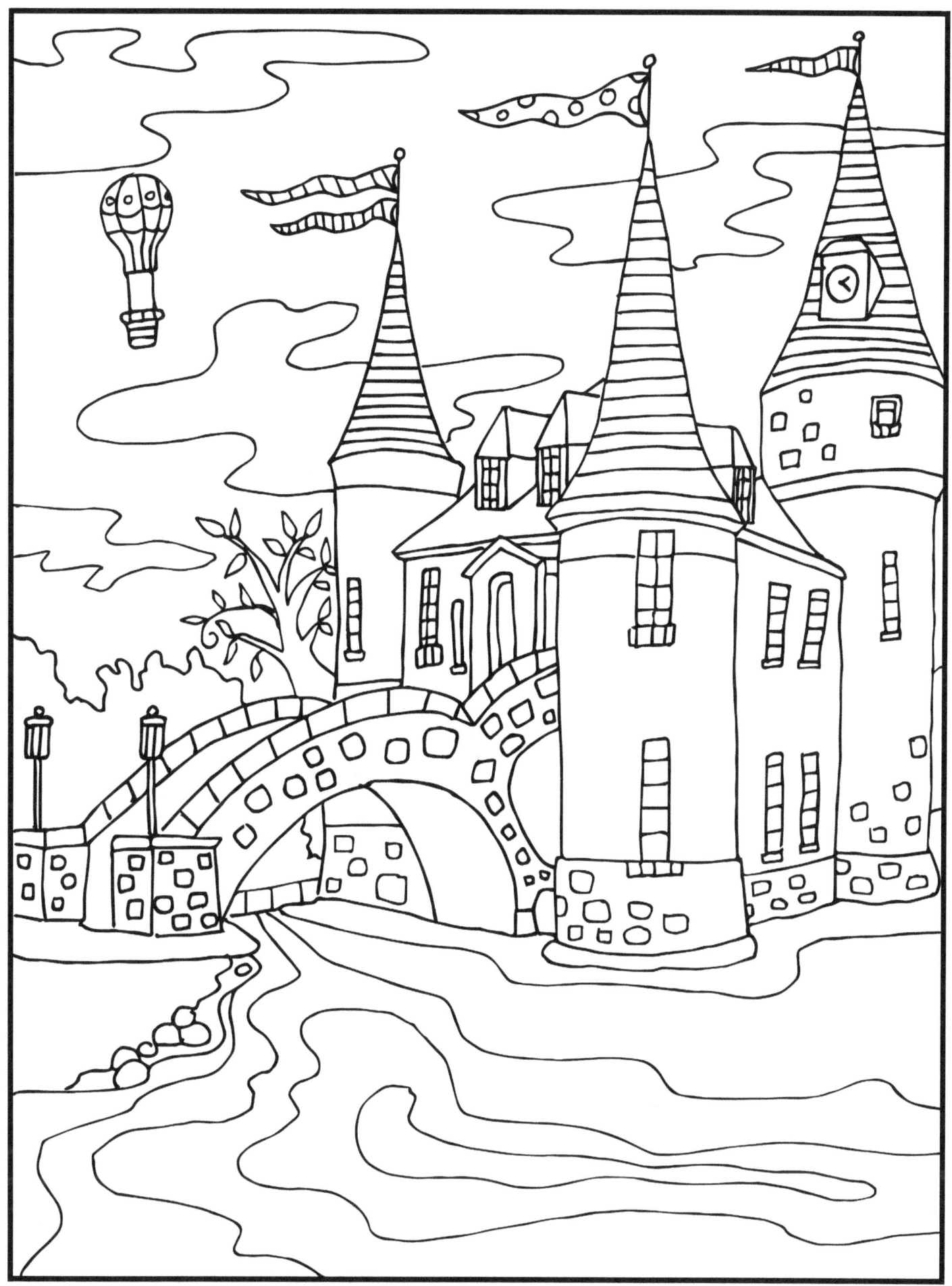

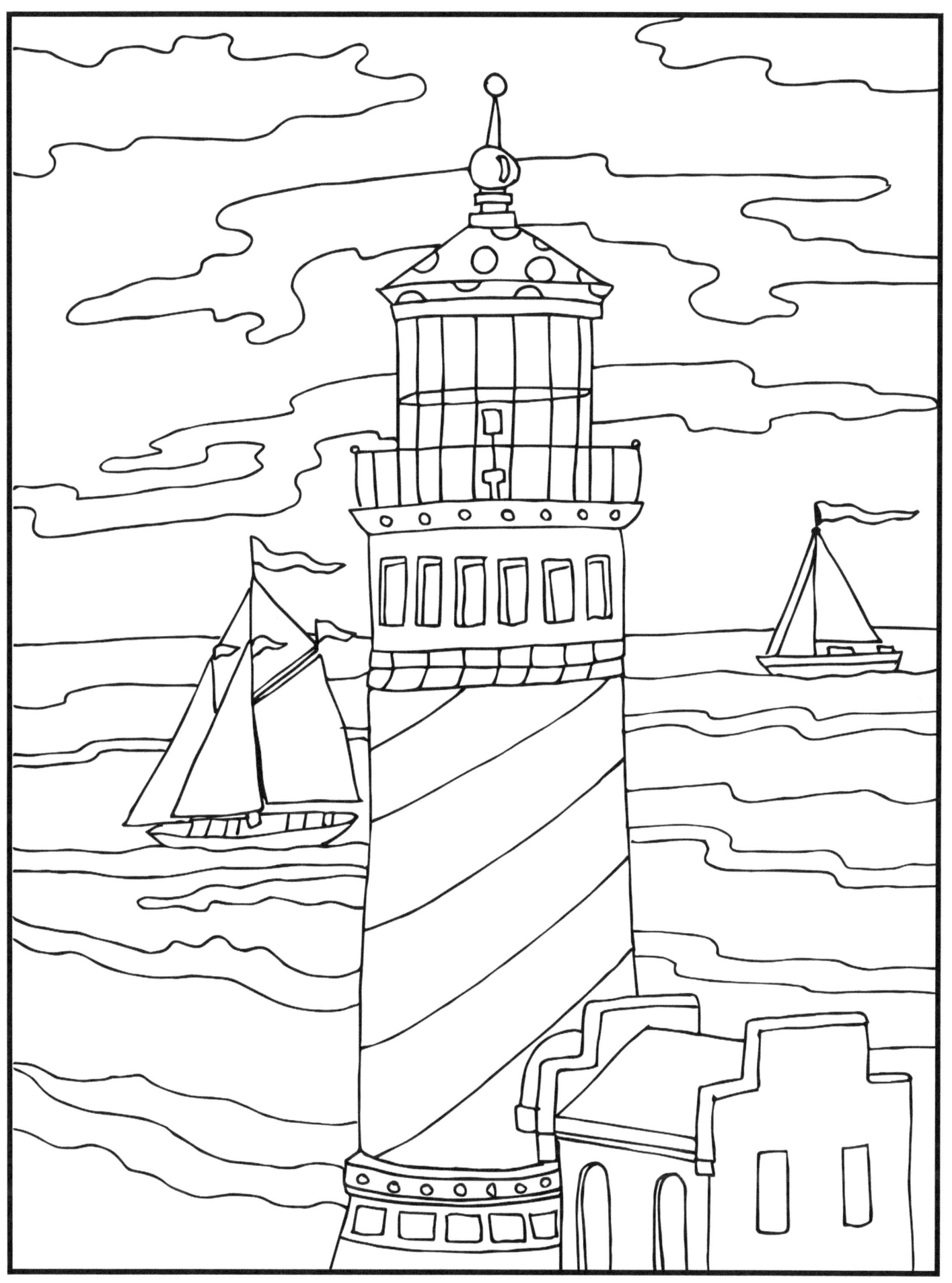

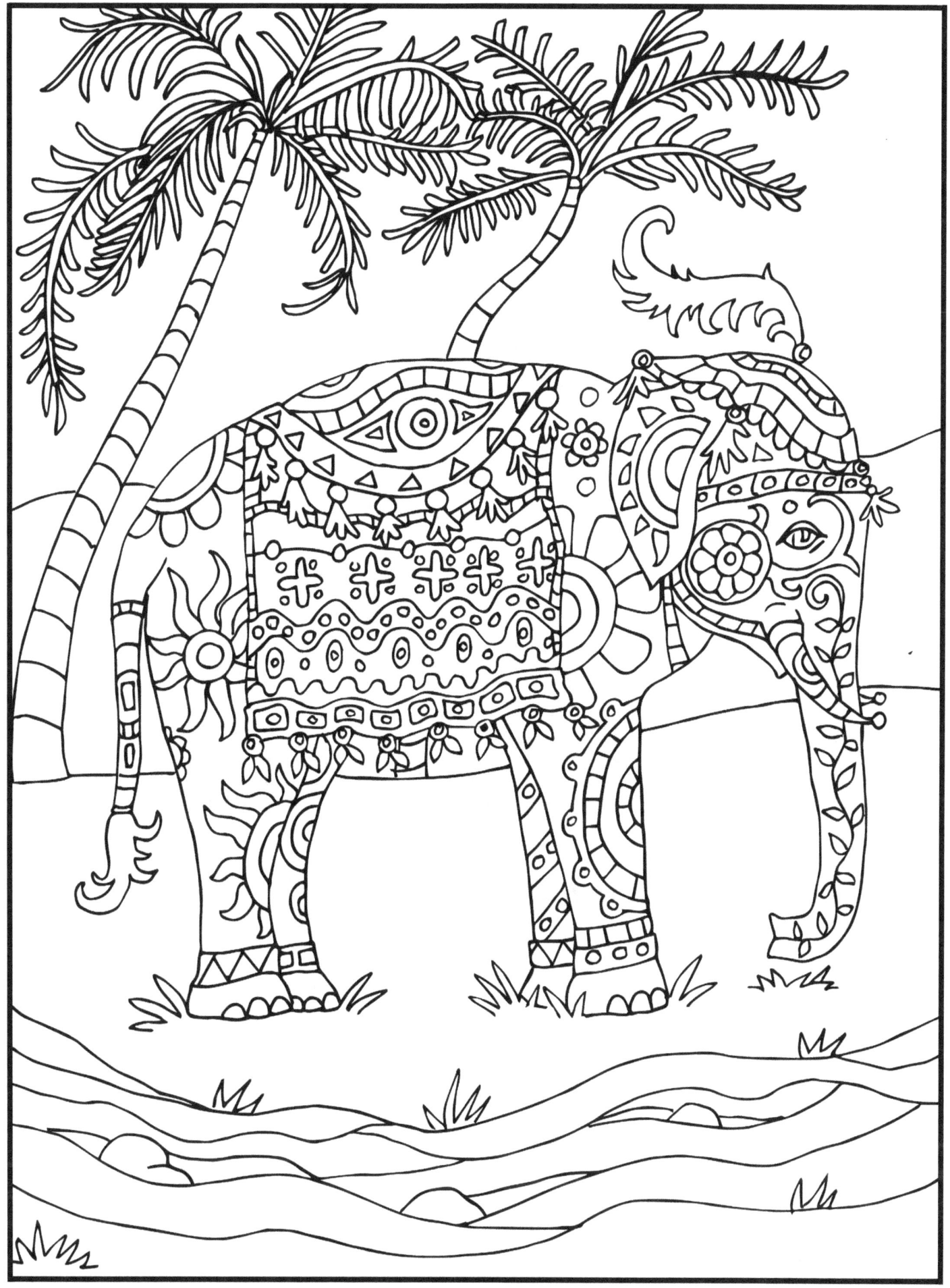

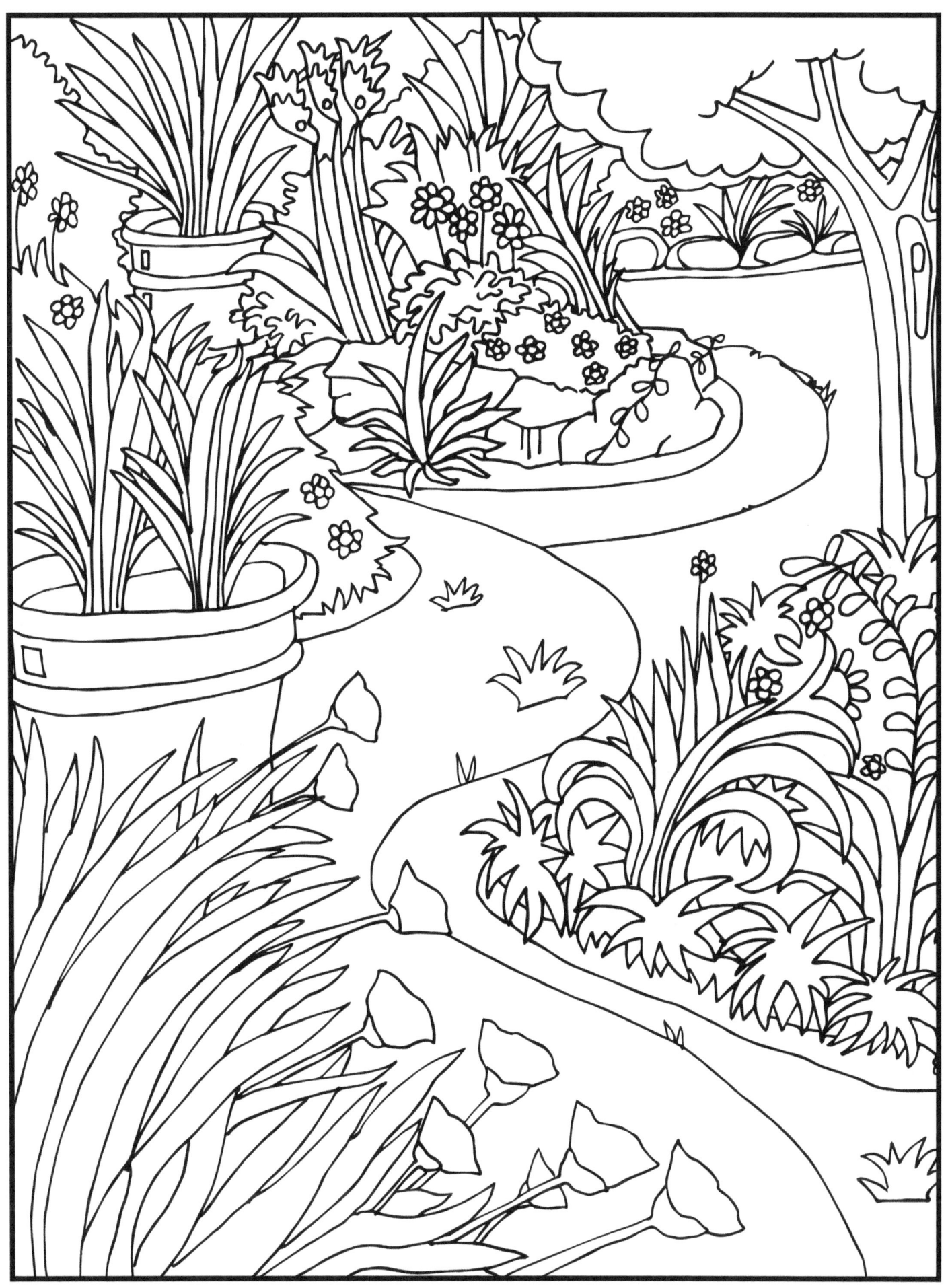

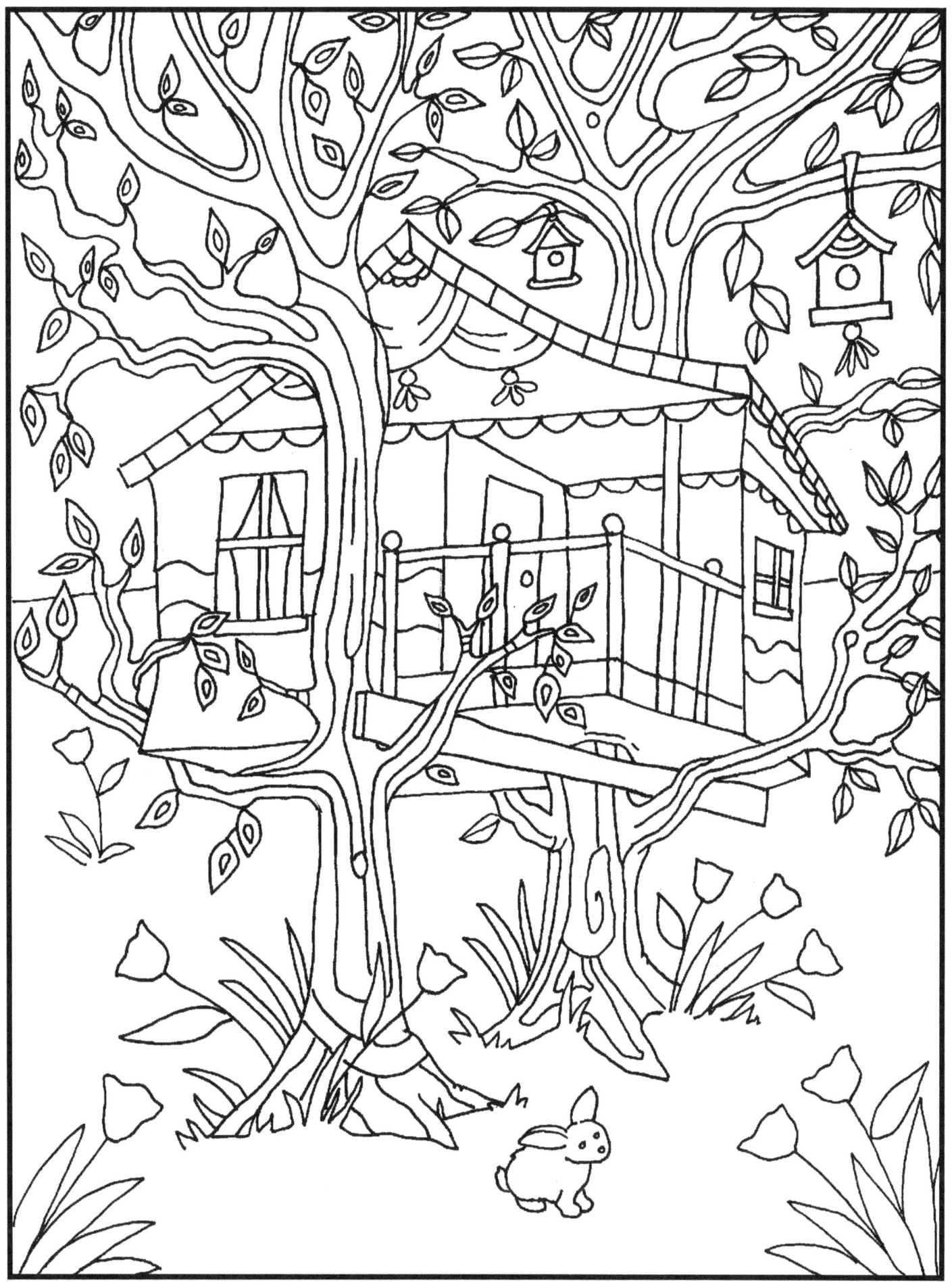

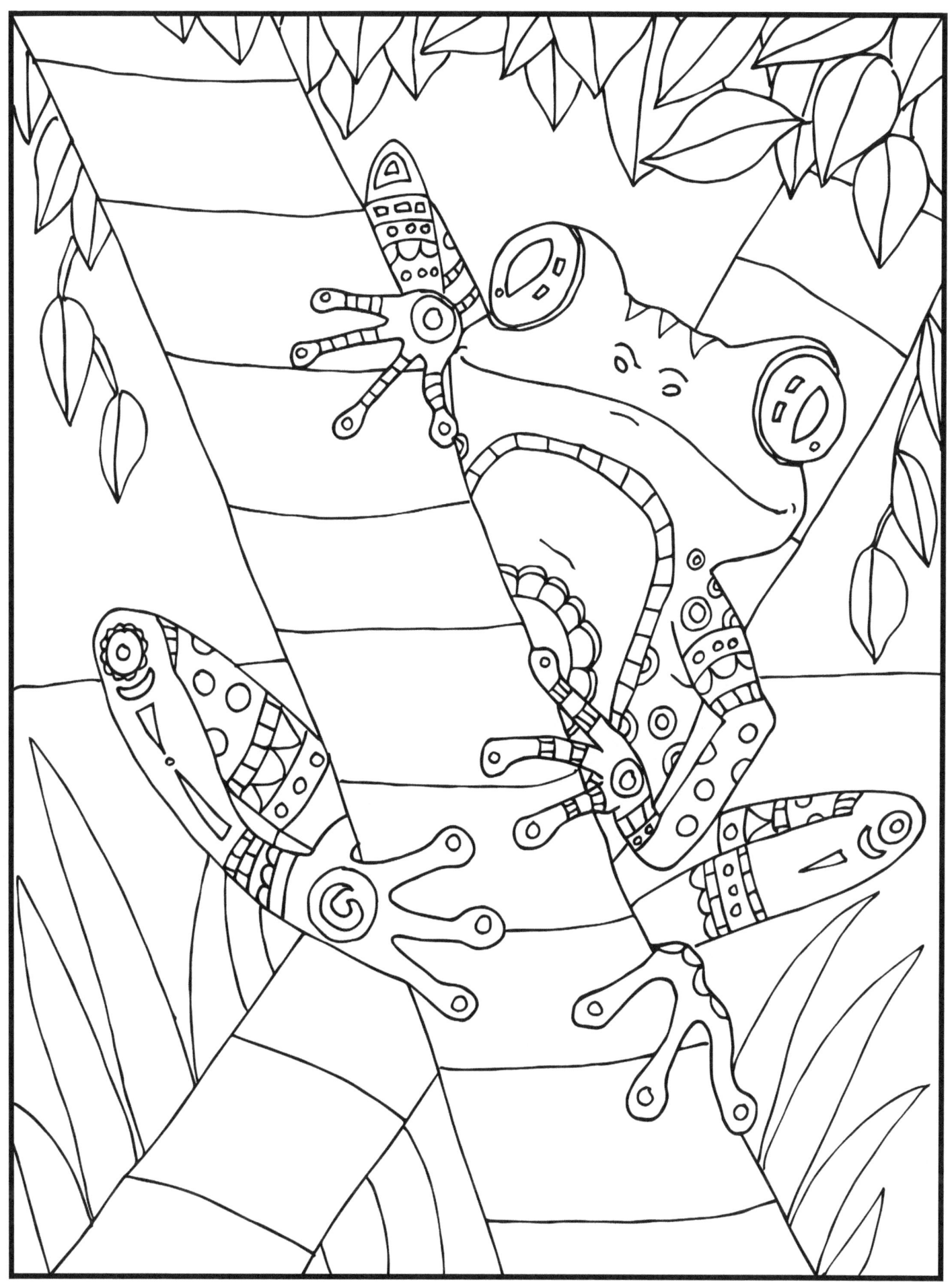

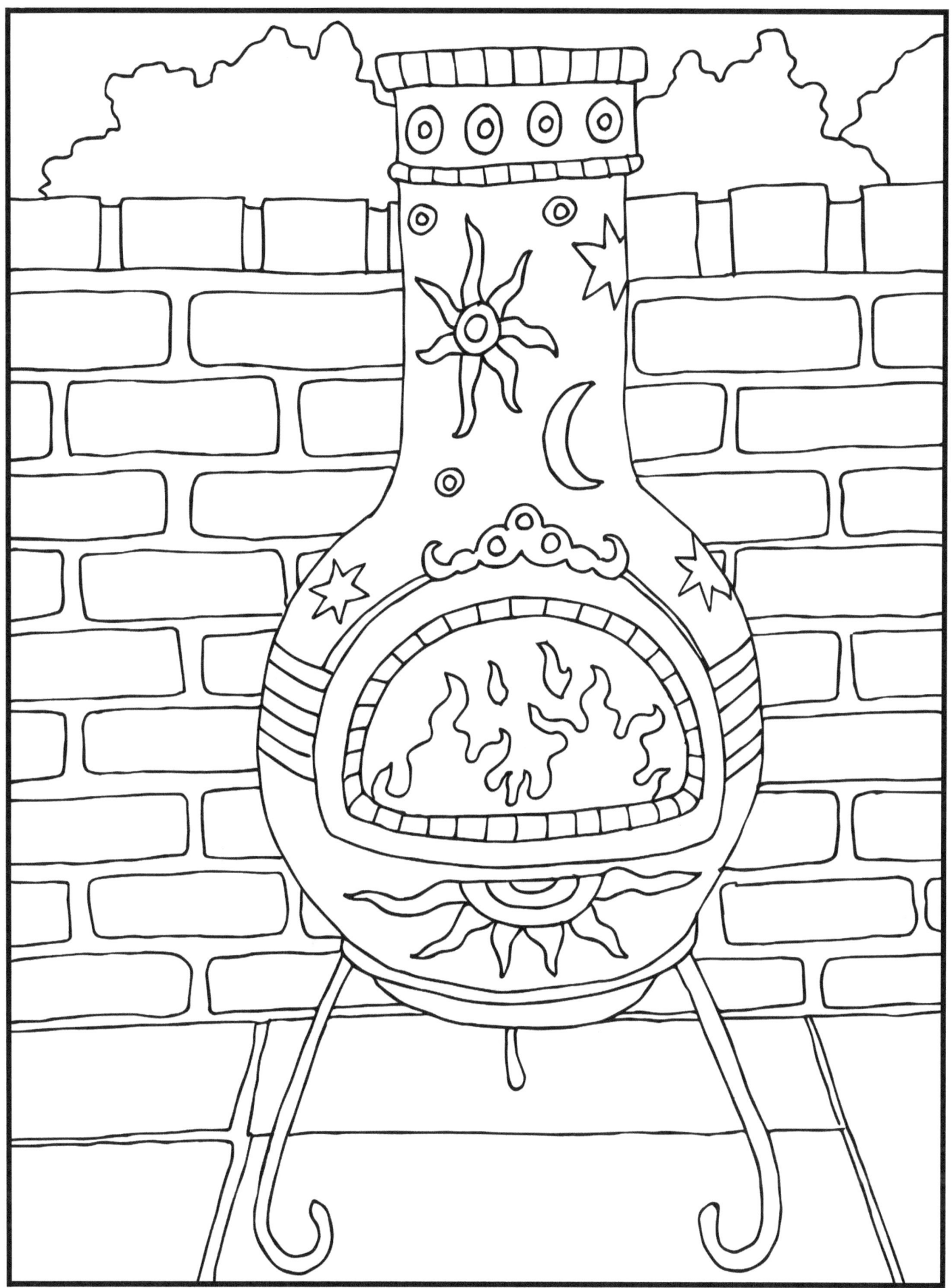

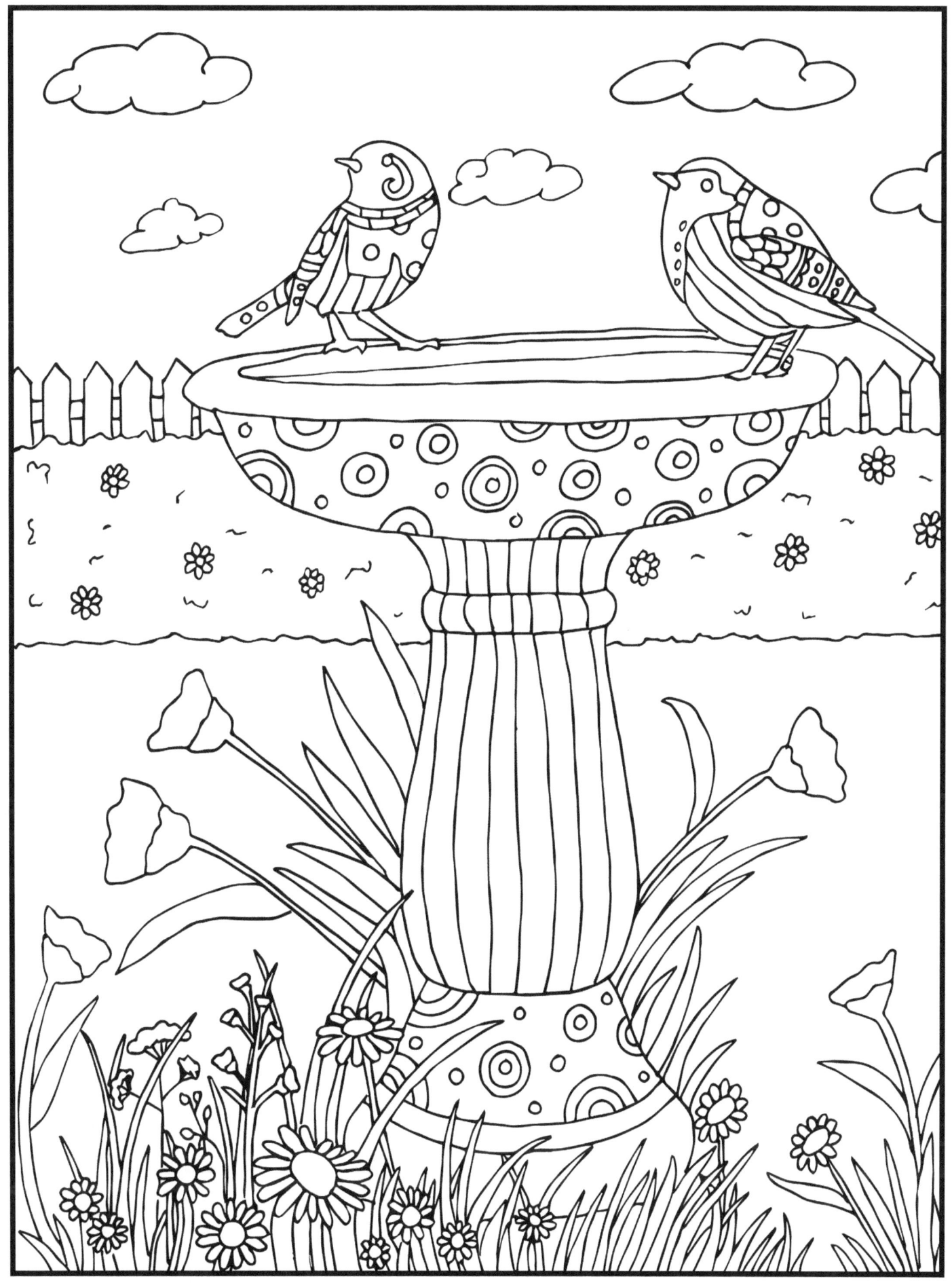

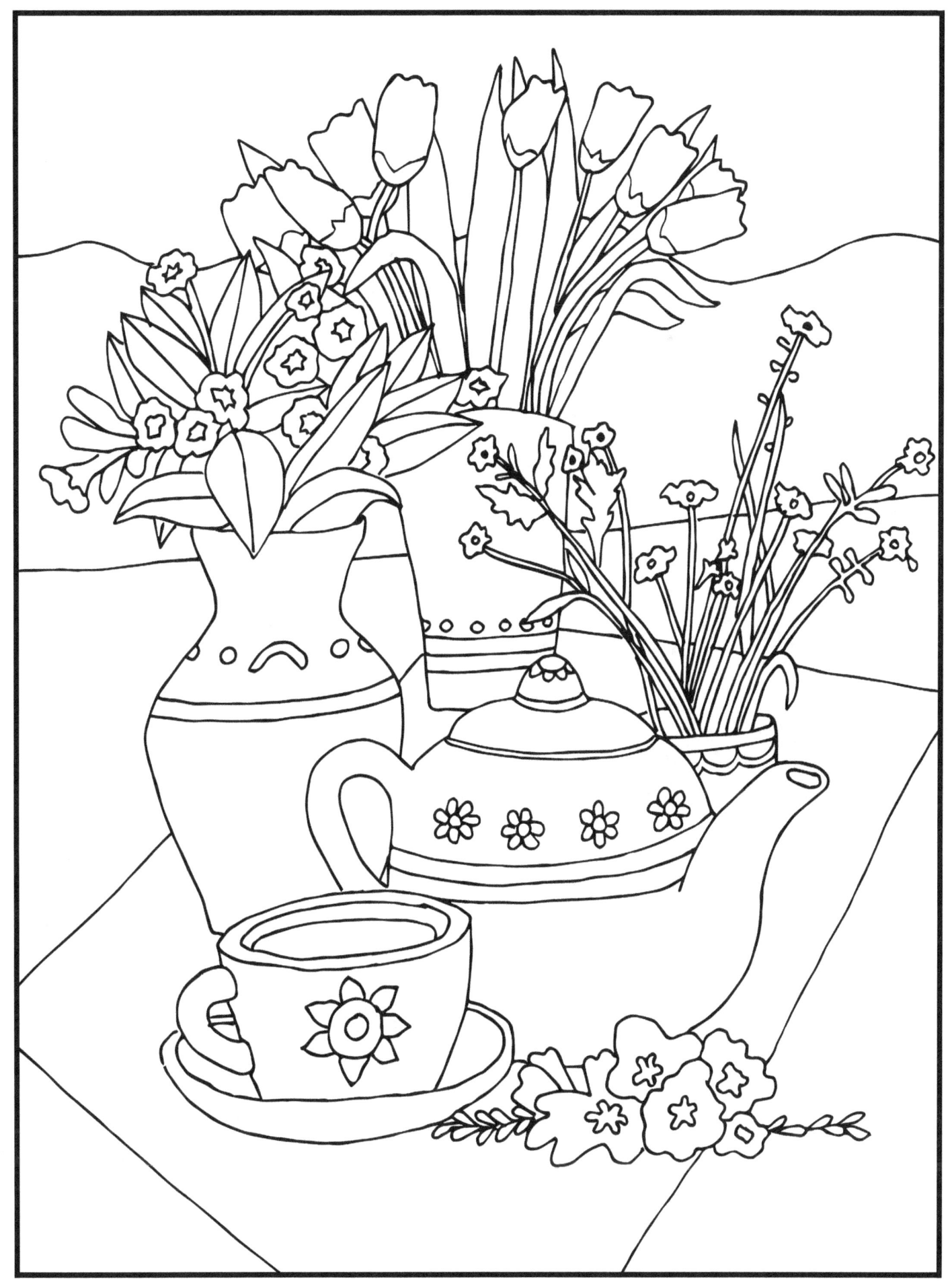

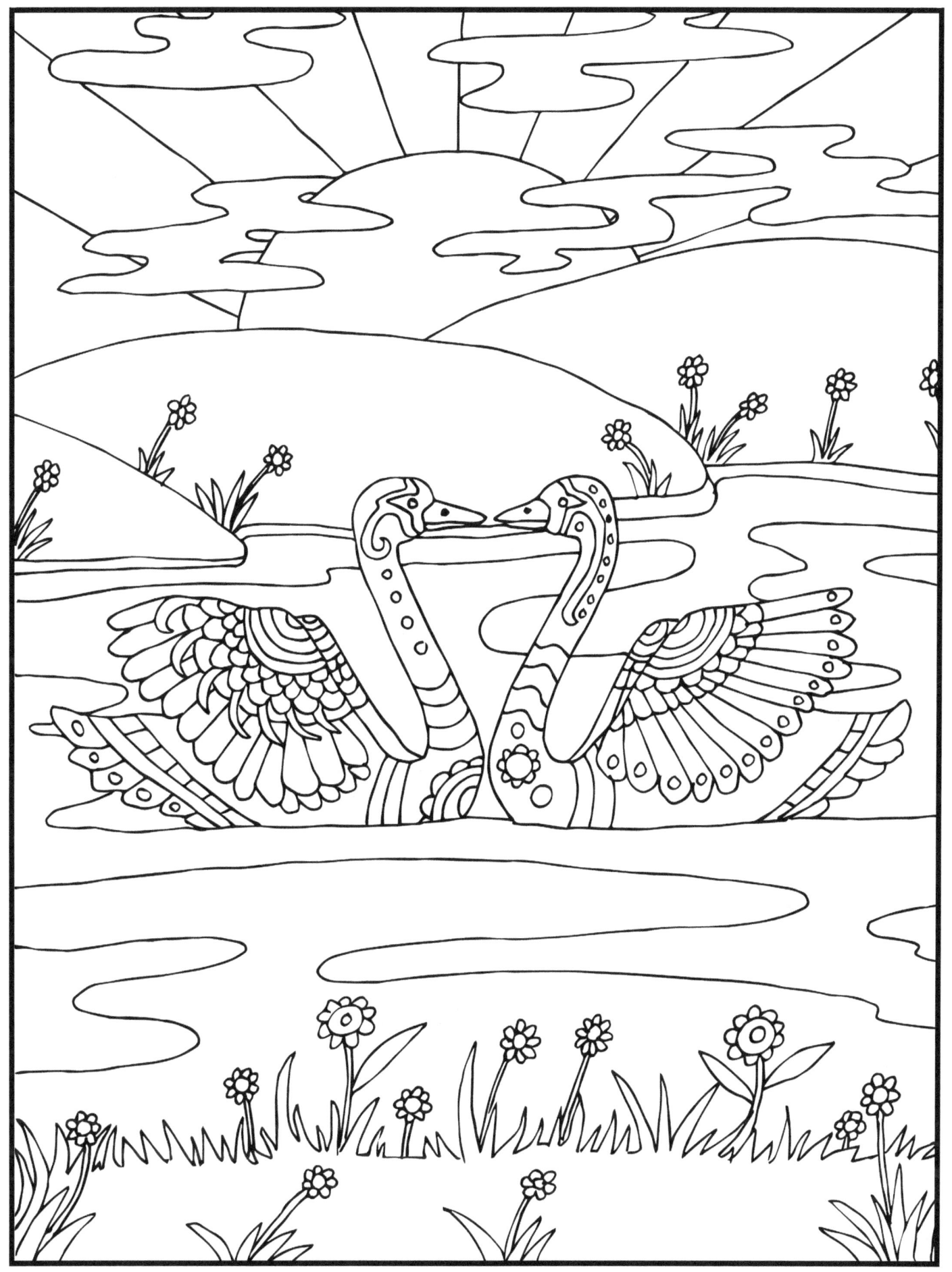

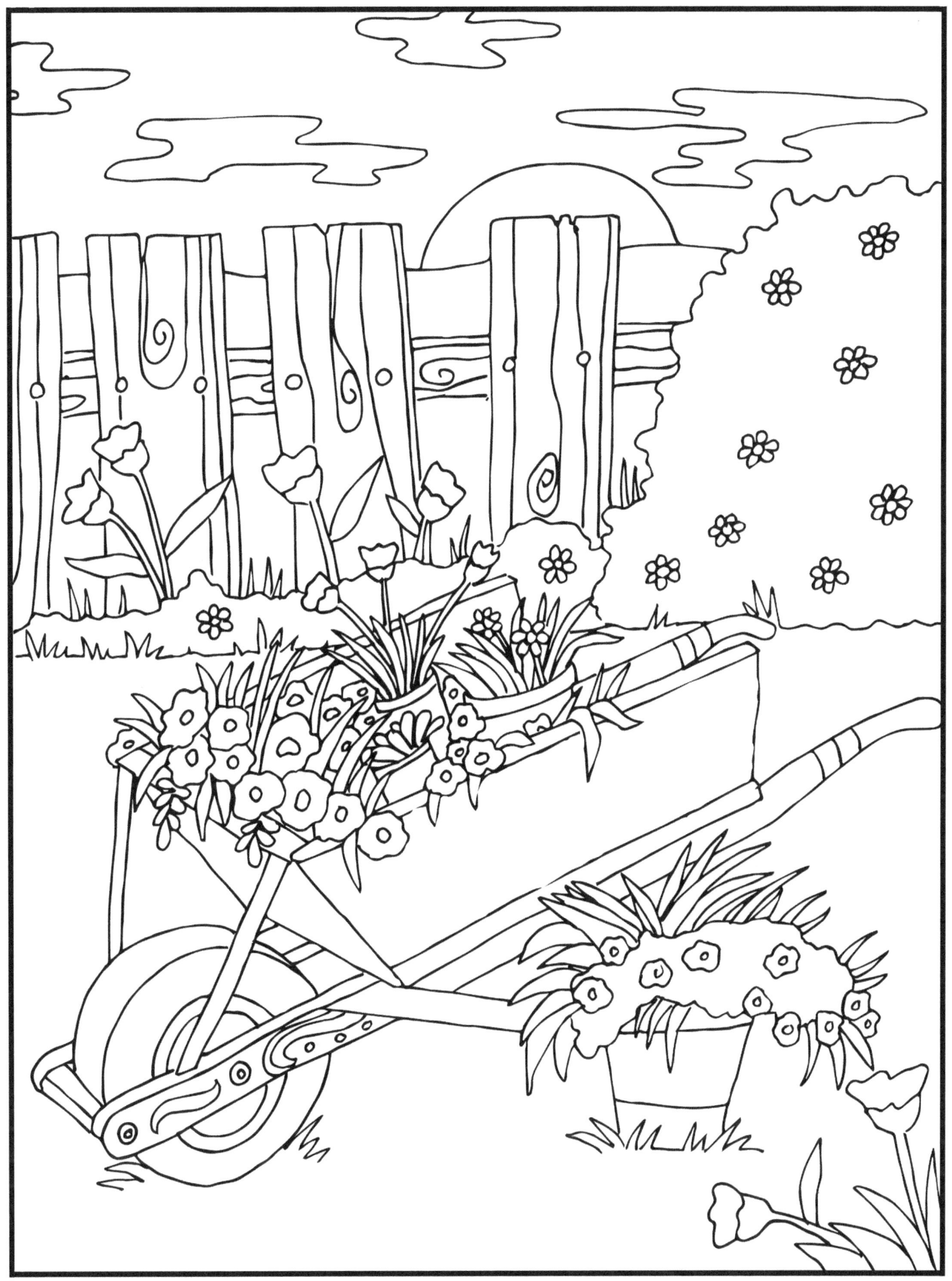

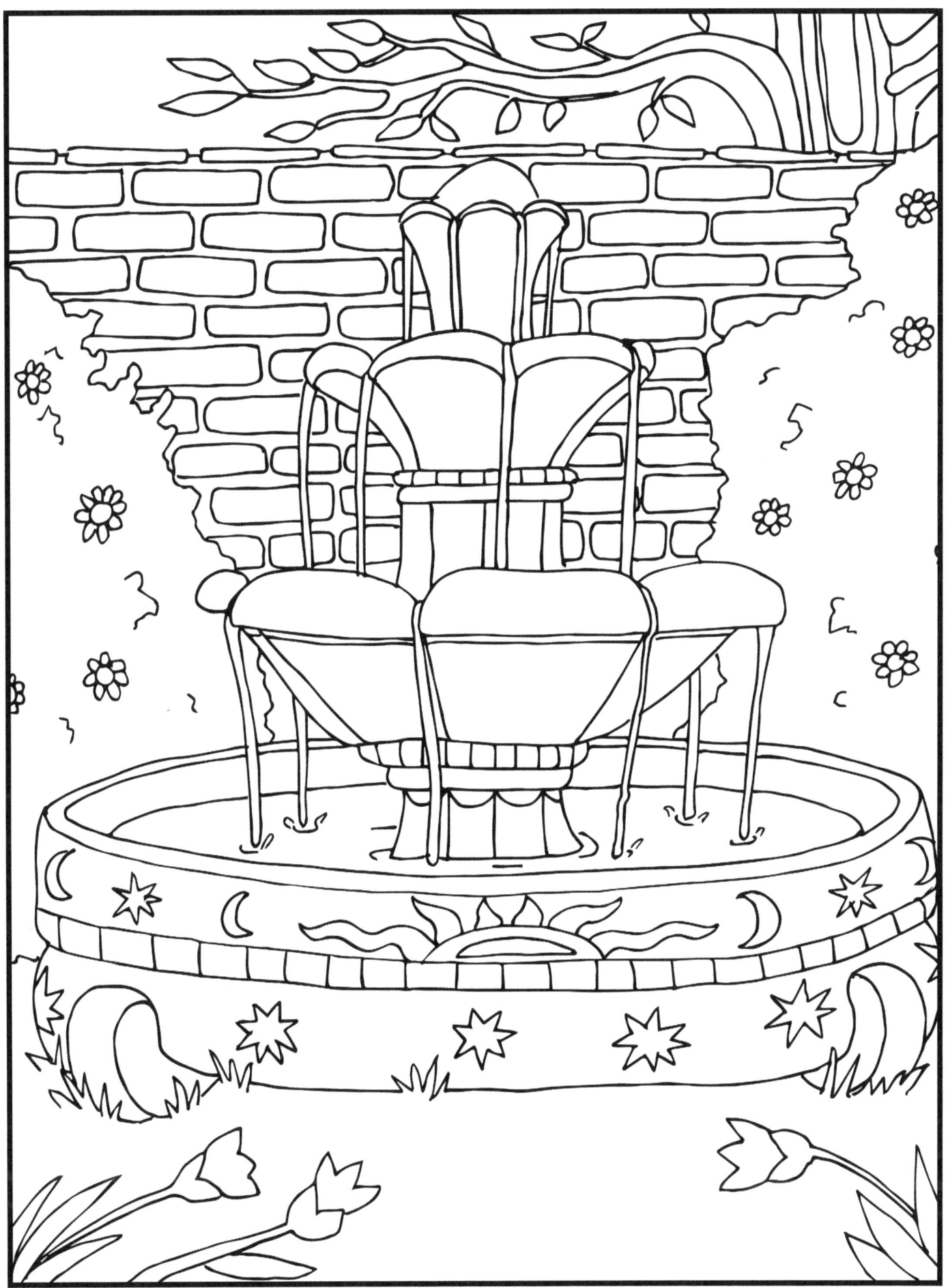

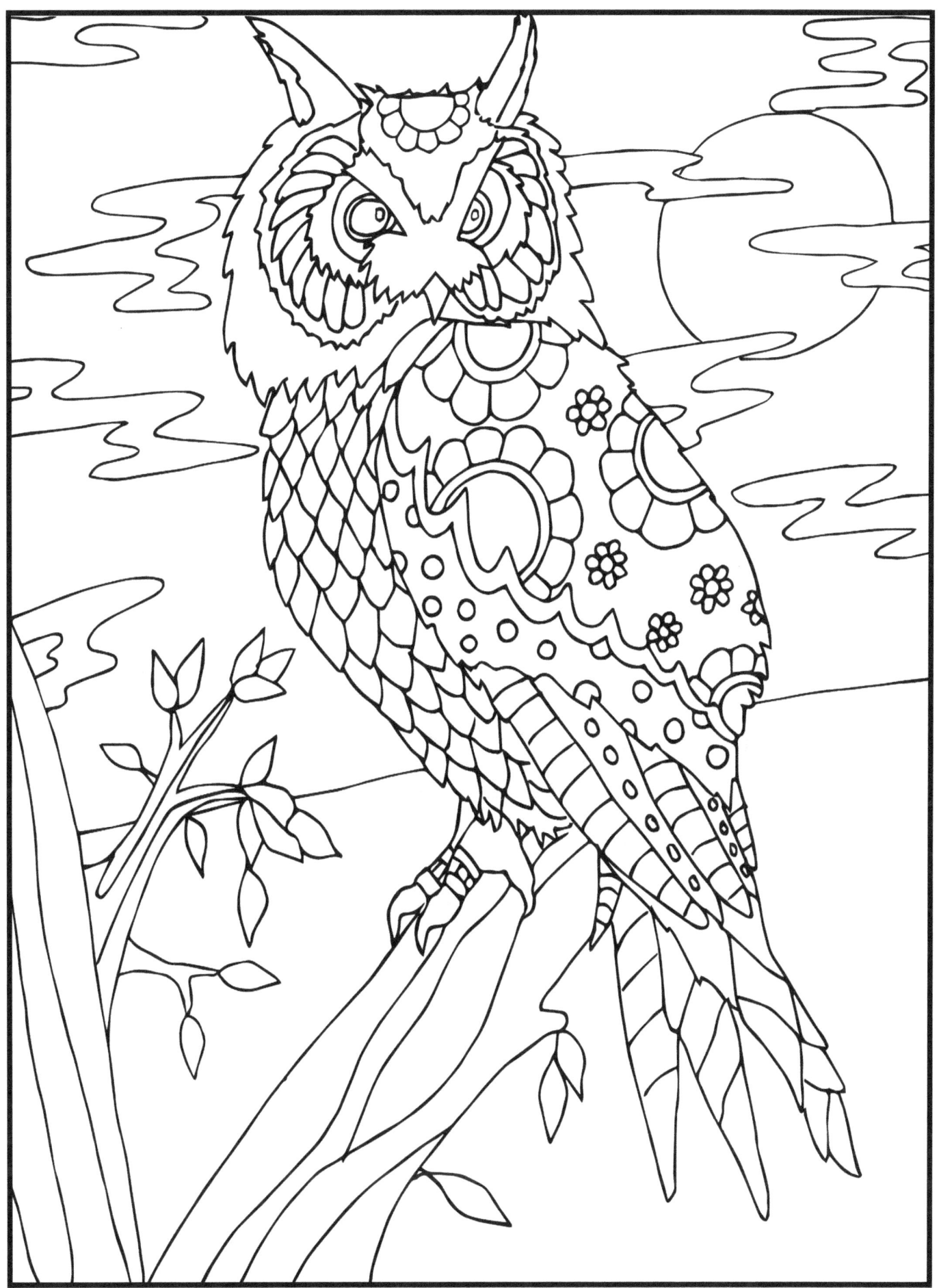

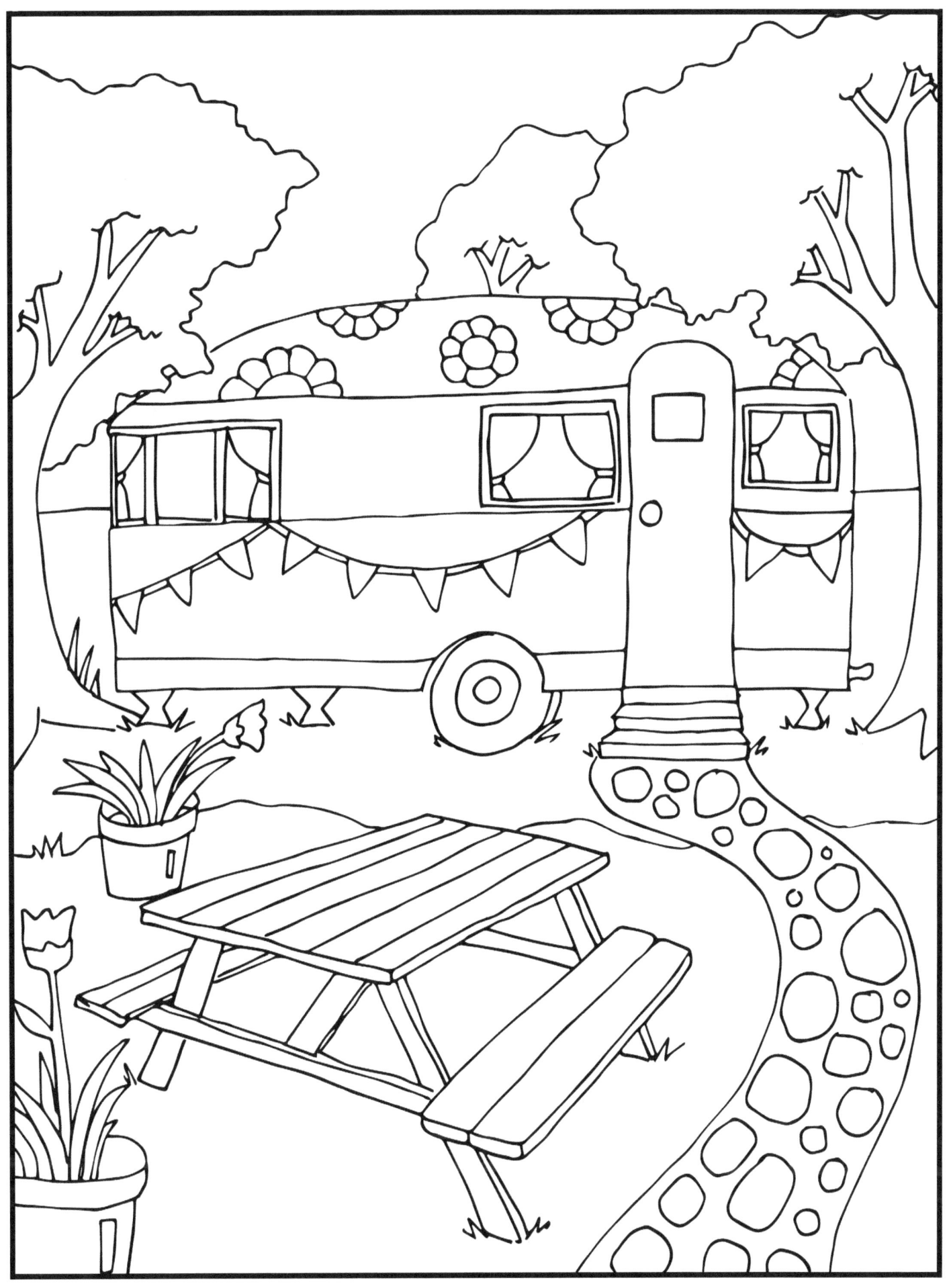

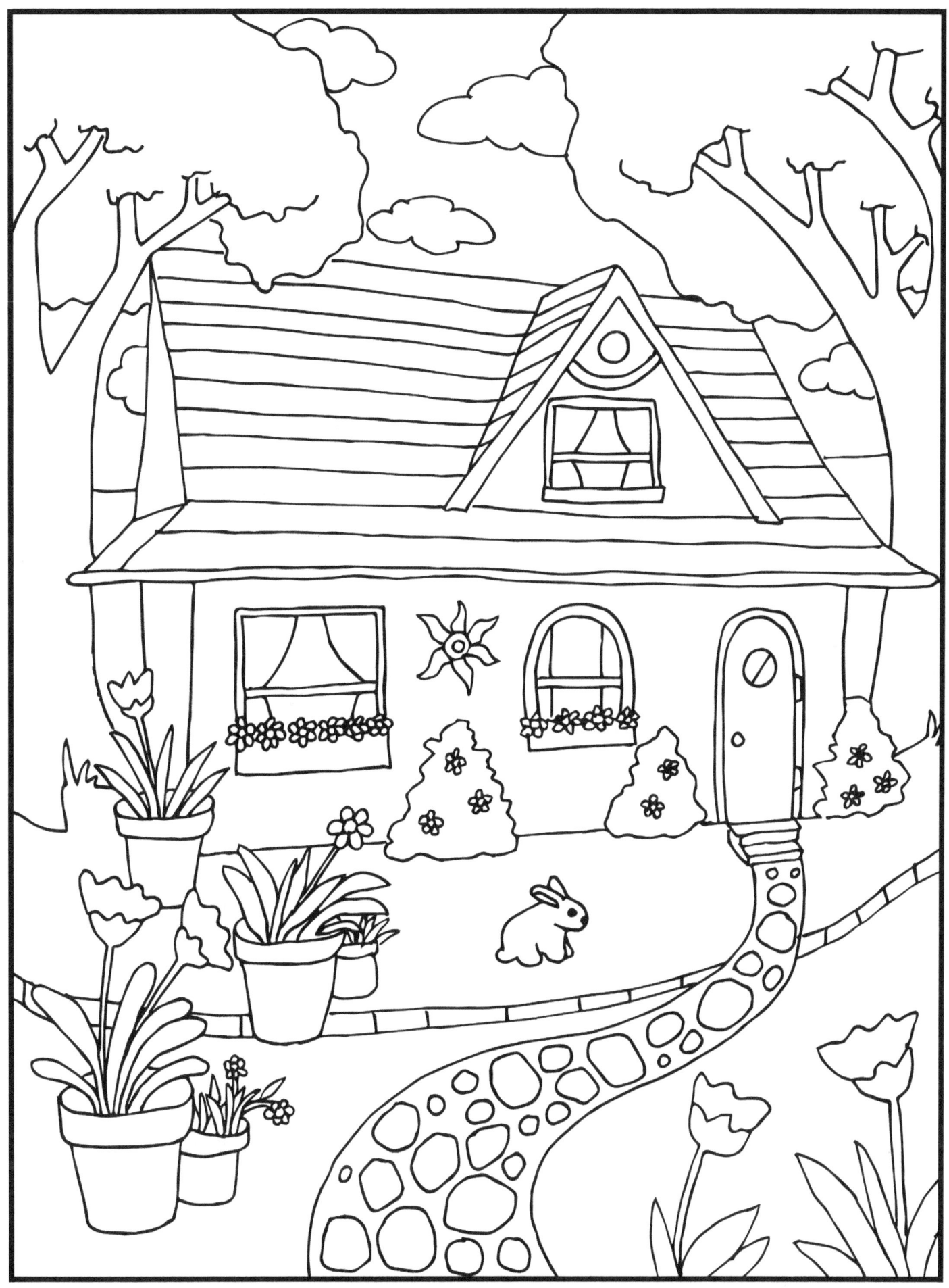

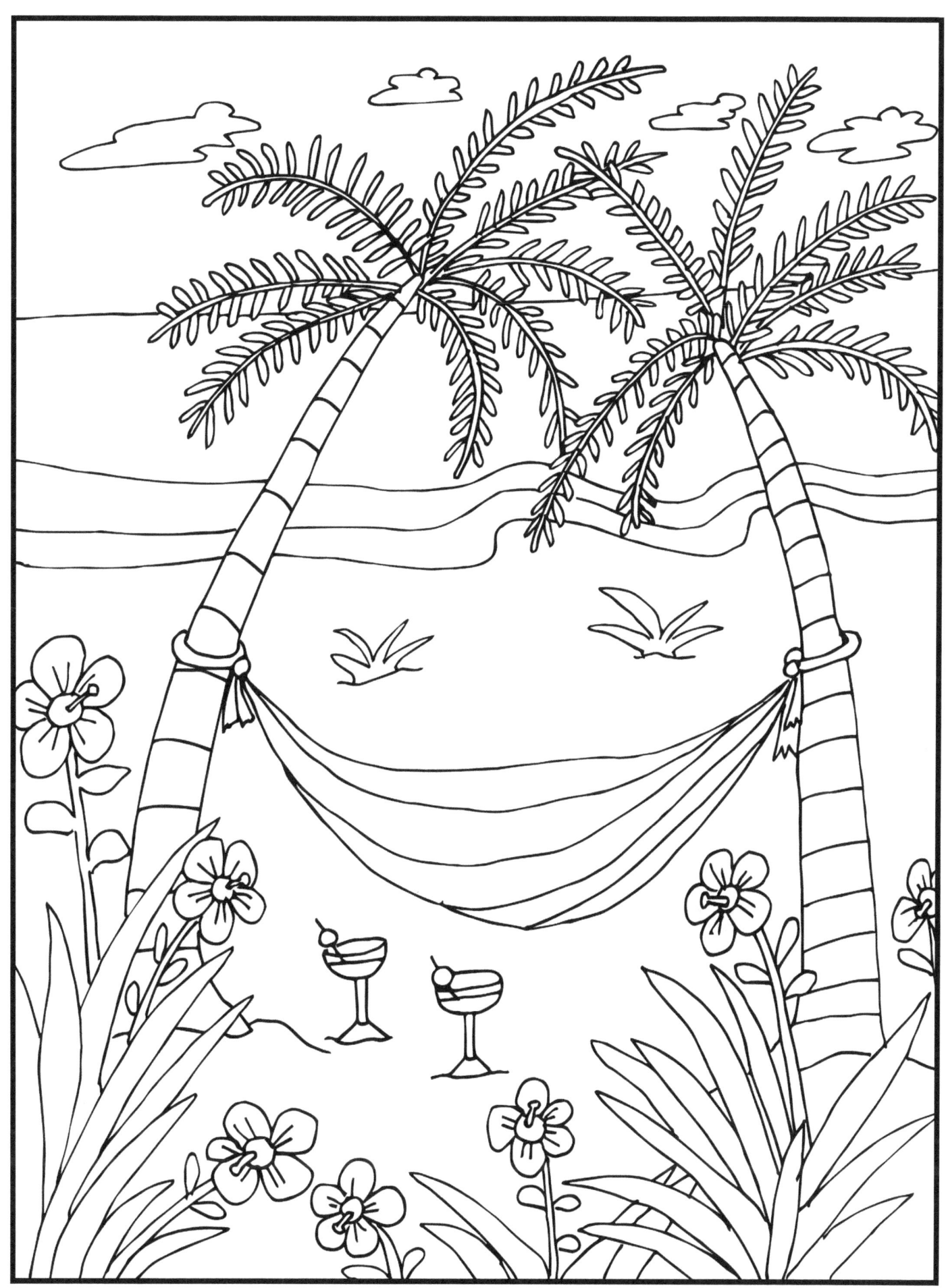

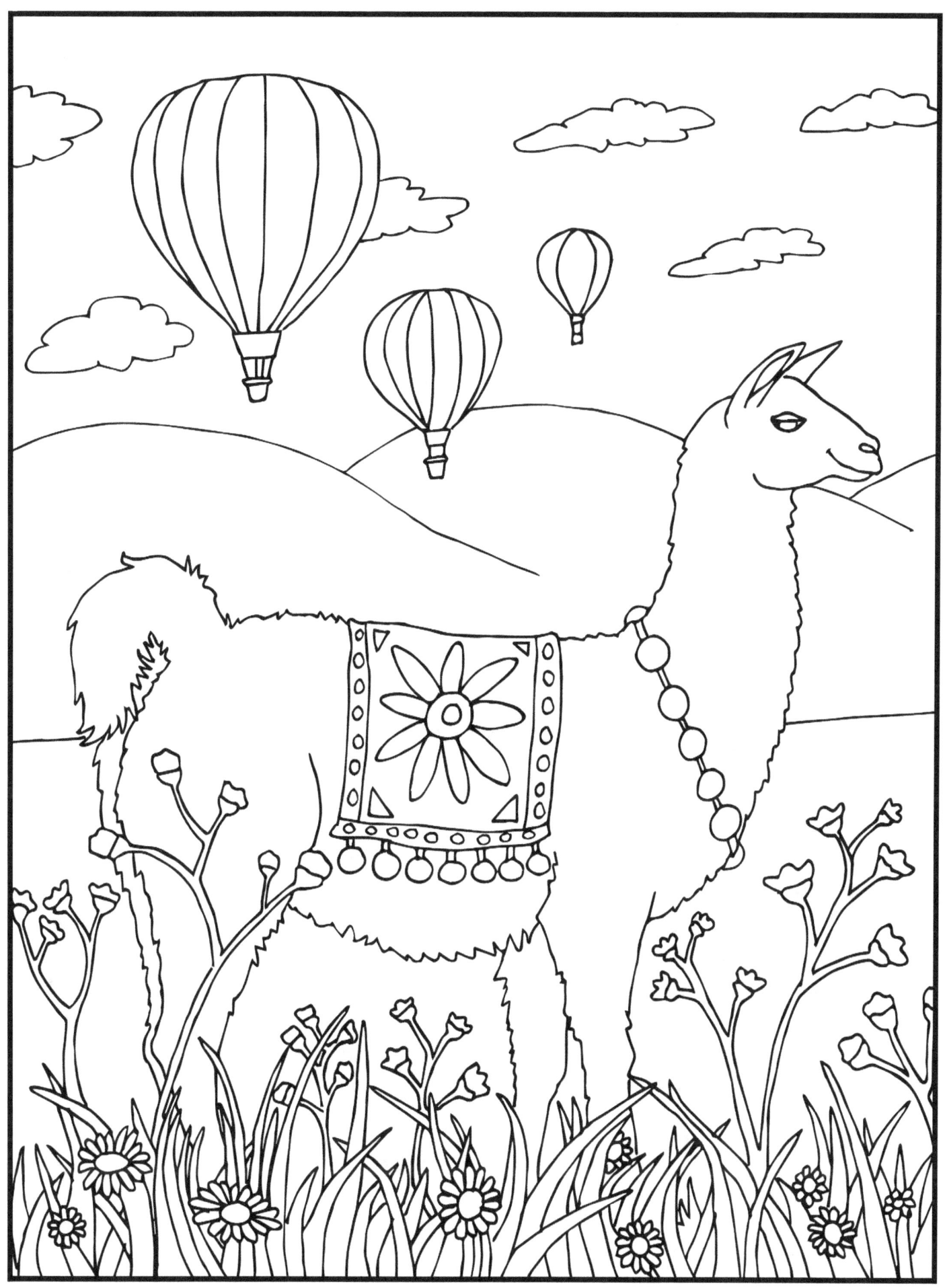

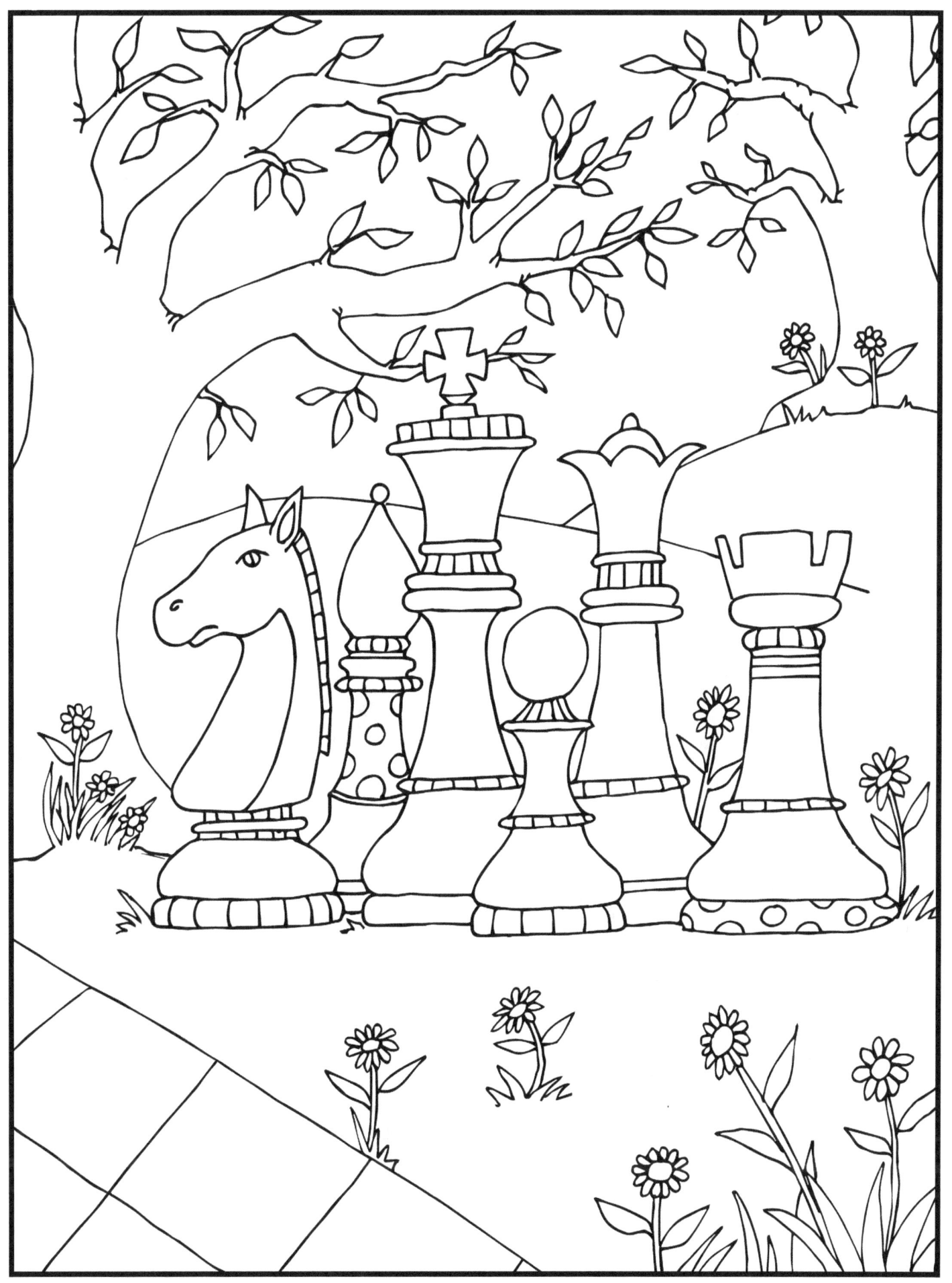

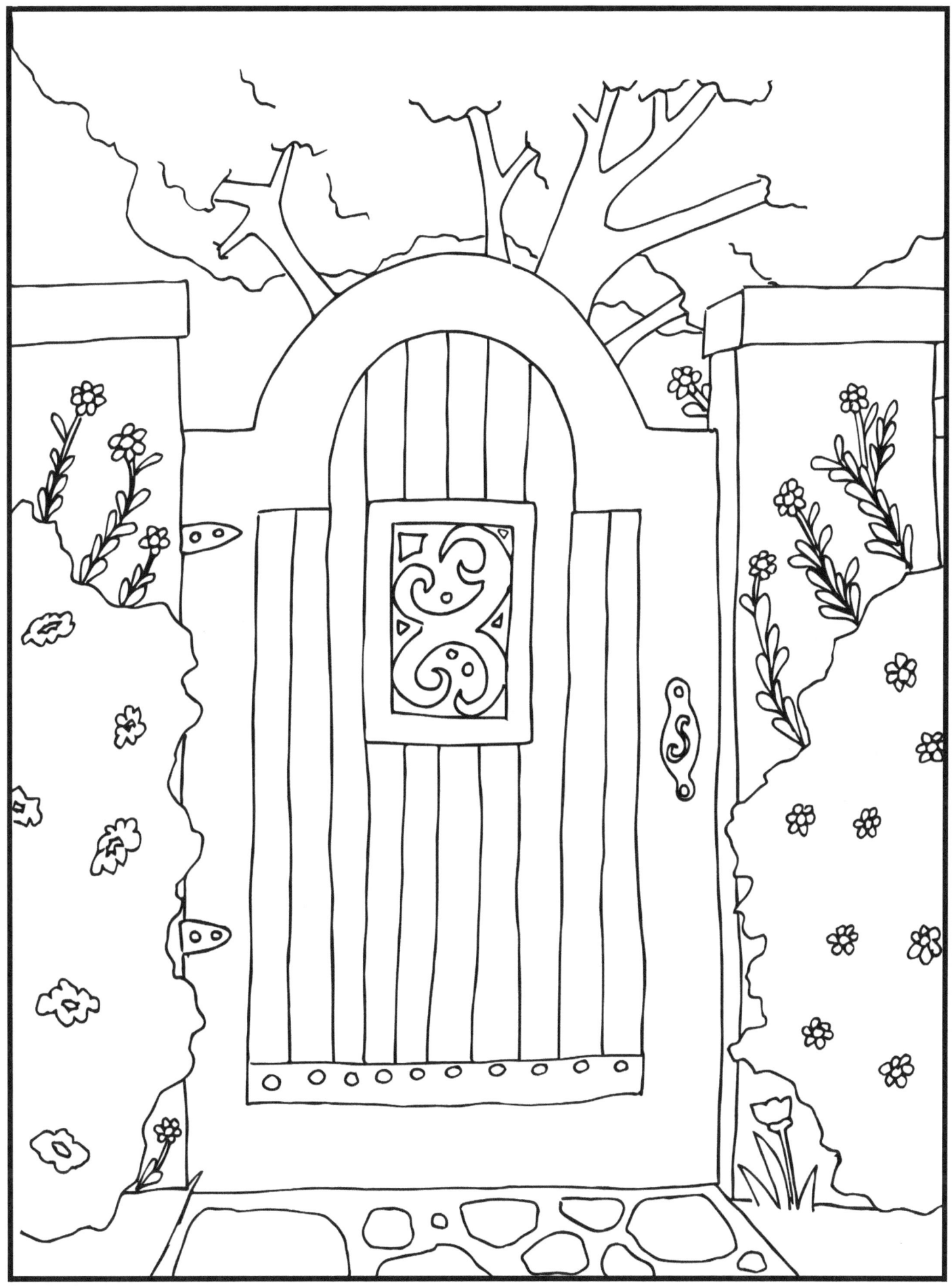

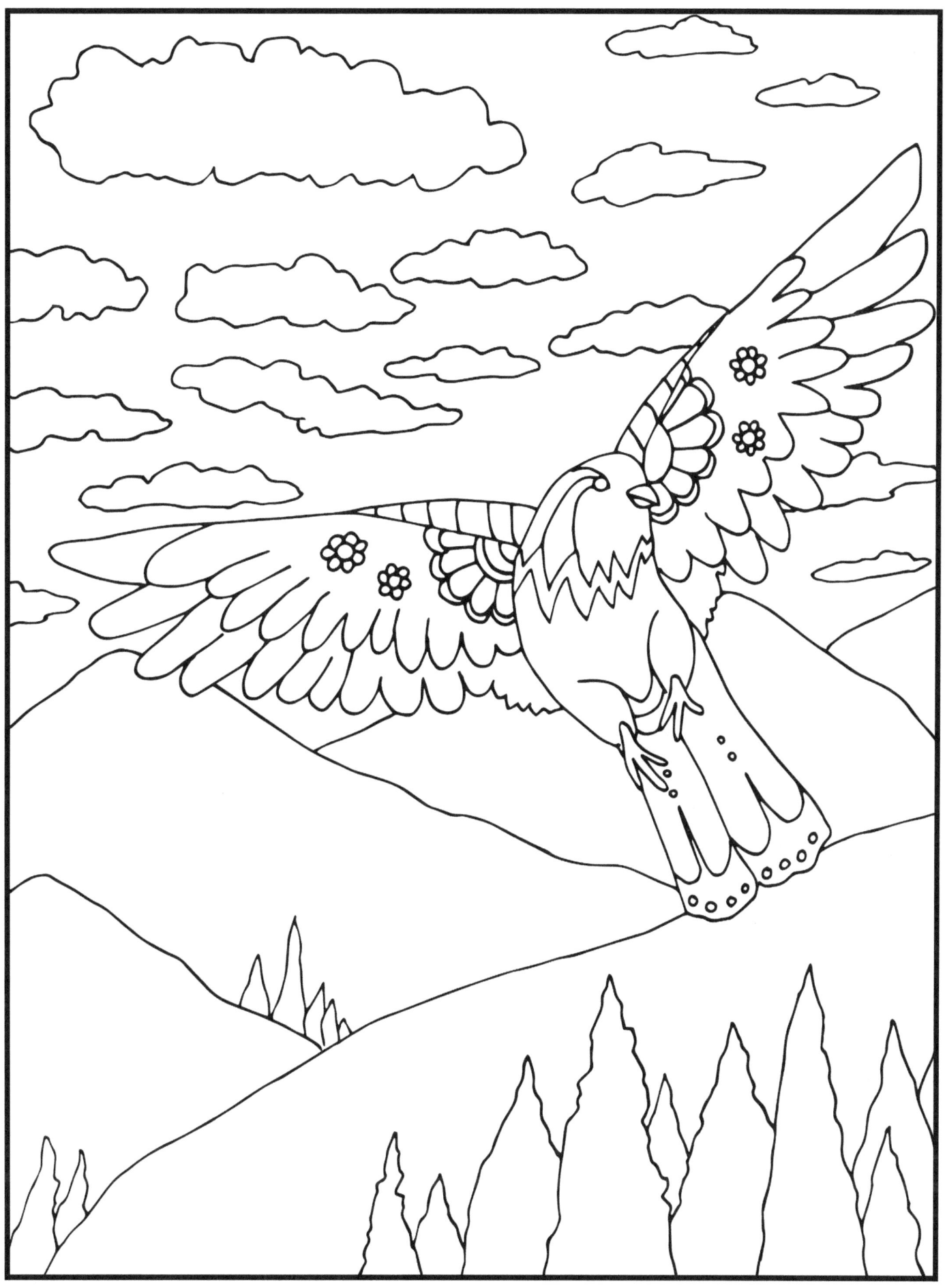

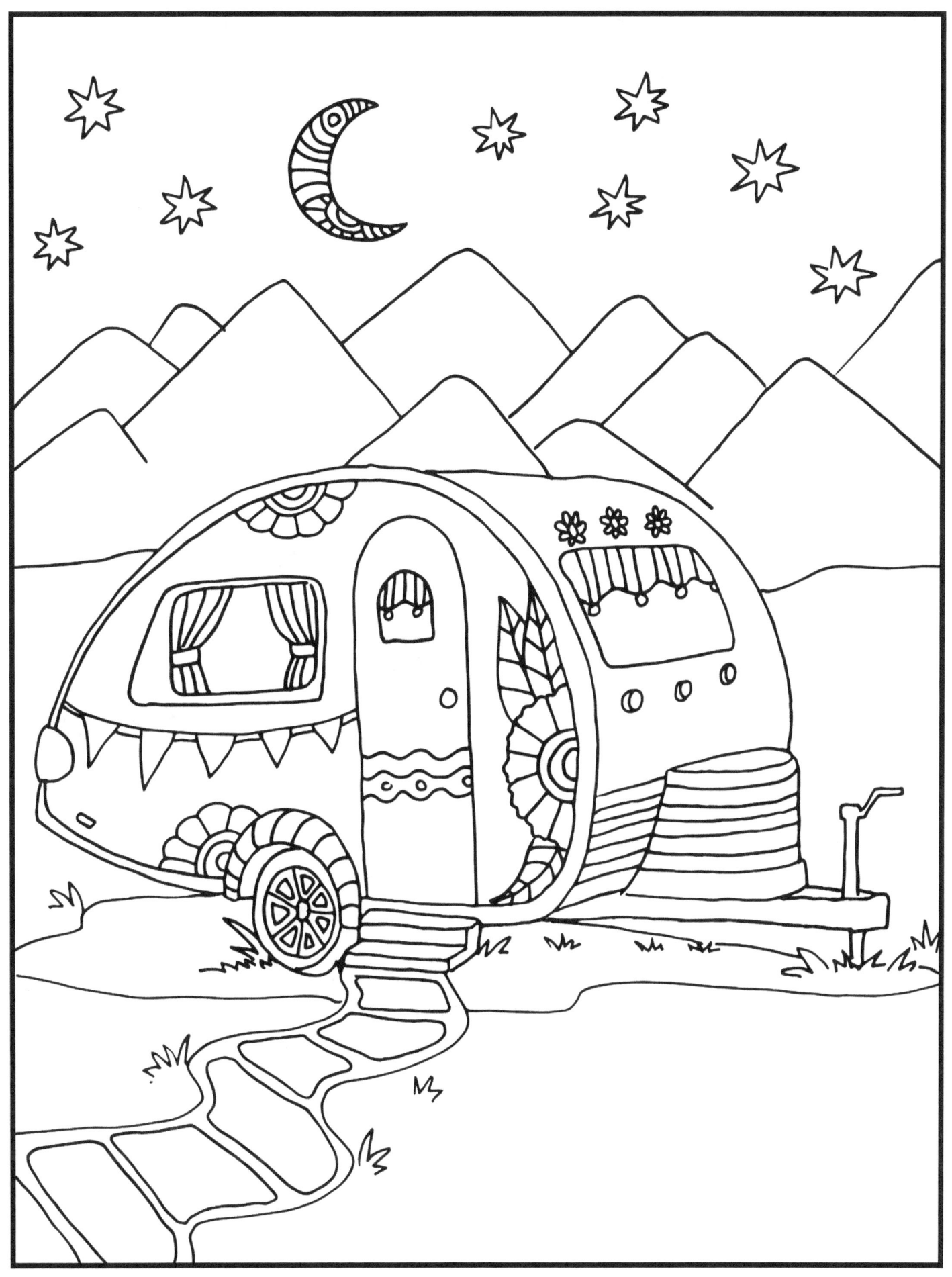

Also Available by Kimberly Garvey

- **Strange Designs** - An adult coloring book for everyone.

- **Strange Little Designs** - A mini/travel adult coloring book.

- **Simple Designs** - An adult coloring book with easier pages.

- **Simple Designs II** - An adult coloring book with easier pages.

- **Simple Little Designs** - A mini/travel sized book w/easier pages.

- **Magical Daydreams** - An adult coloring book for everyone.

- **It's Complicated** - A challenging, more detailed book for the daring colorists.

- **The Fox Book** - A foxy coloring book for everyone.

- **SUPER Simple Designs -** SUPER easy adult coloring

- **Playful Adventures** - An adult coloring book for everyone.

- **Random Designs** - Designs of various difficulty levels.

- **Alien Flowers From Another Dimension** - An adult coloring book for everyone.

- **I Love Hearts** - Heart themed coloring book for all.

- **Hours of Flowers** - An adult flowery coloring book.

KIMBERLYGARVEY.COM

PROTECTION SHEET

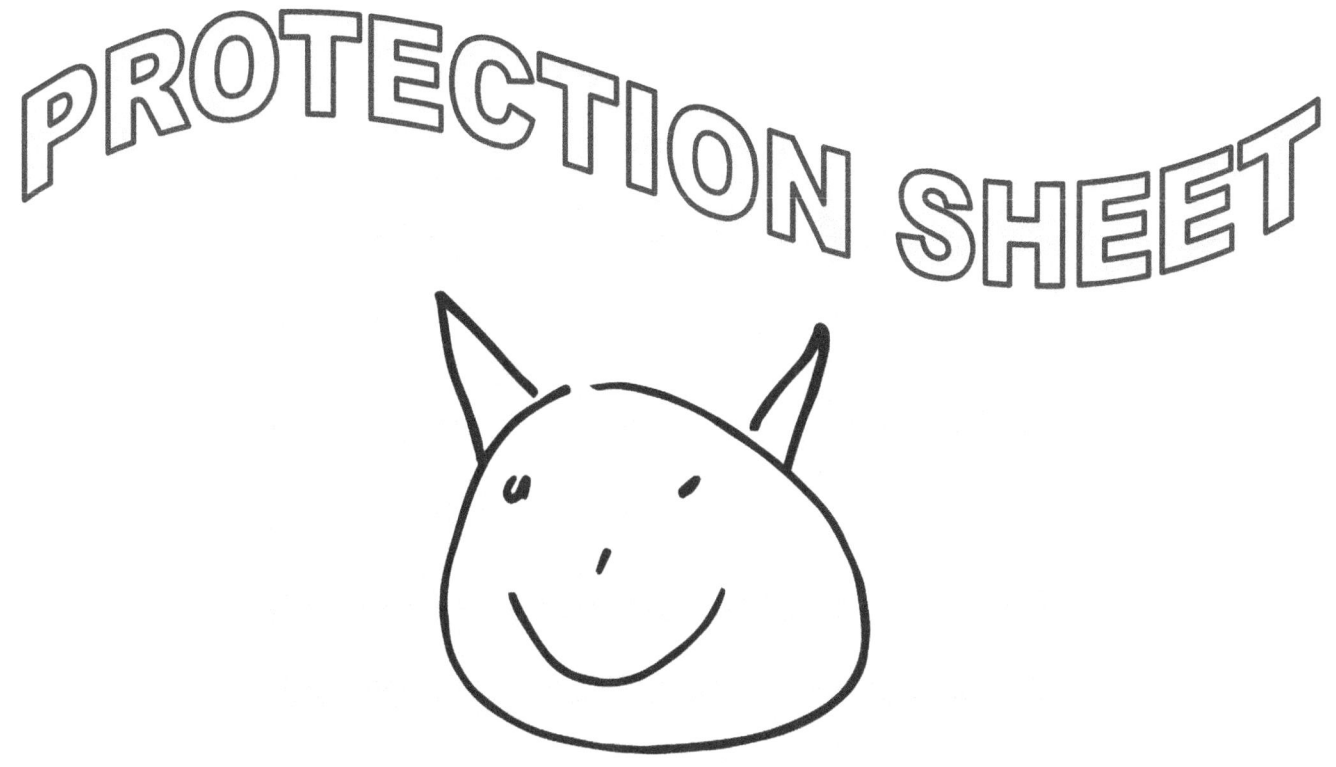

Place this page between coloring pages when using markers to prevent bleed-through.